Barry Richards on Cricket

Attack to Win

Barry Richards on Cricket

Attack to Win

with a Foreword by
SIR DONALD BRADMAN

Pelham Books

First published in Great Britain by
PELHAM BOOKS LTD
52 Bedford Square, London, W.C.1
1973

© 1973 by Barry Richards

All Rights Reserved. No part of this publication
may be recorded, stored in a retrieval system,
or transmitted, in any form or by any means,
electronic, mechanical, photocopying, recording
or otherwise, without the prior permission
of the Copyright owner

ISBN 0 7207 0583 5

*Set and printed in Great Britain by
Tonbridge Printers Ltd, Peach Hall Works, Tonbridge, Kent
in Times eleven on twelve and a half point on paper supplied by
P. F. Bingham Ltd, and bound by James Burn
at Esher, Surrey*

Acknowledgements

I wish to acknowledge my great debt to Martin Tyler in writing this book. His help, advice and literary expertise alone made it possible.

The action photographs in the book, and the cover photograph are by Patrick Eagar to whom my thanks are also due.

Contents

	Foreword by Sir Donald Bradman	11
1.	Comfort at the Crease	13
2.	Defensive Technique	20
3.	Attack off the Front Foot	28
4.	Attack off the Back Foot	41
5.	Building an Innings	51
6.	The Basics of Bowling	60
7.	Fast and Medium Pace Bowling	68
8.	Spin Bowling	78
9.	Wicket Taking	87
10.	The Techniques of Fielding	93
11.	Wicket-Keeping	101
12.	The Responsibilities of the Skipper	107
13.	Equipment	113
14.	Approach to the Game	120
	Index	125

Illustrations

Between Pages 16 and 17
1. The grip... fundamental to correct batting technique
2. A rare moment of defence for Essex's Brian Taylor
3. The backward defensive shot
4. Even when there is more aggression in a shot the bat should come straight down wherever possible
5. The off drive, the classic front-foot attacking shot
6. Never be afraid to go down the wicket and drive the ball over the top

Between Pages 48 and 49
7. Peter Sainsbury 'works' the ball on the leg-side
8. The sweep, the ideal way to attack an off spinner on a turning wicket
9. The pull
10. The square cut, the perfect answer to a short ball outside the off stump
11. The cut is not exclusively a back-foot shot
12. Perhaps the only time the old-fashioned heave can truly be justified
13. The author found leg-side shots difficult to master when he first played county cricket

Between Pages 80 and 81
14. Text-book action from Australian fast bowler, Dennis Lillee
15. Mike Procter has achieved success at the highest levels bowling off the 'wrong' foot
16. A follow-through is an essential part of delivering the ball
17. Alan Knott attempts to stump Ian Chappell
18. Peter Parfitt plunges to catch Bob Massie, Third Test, 1972

Diagrams

		Page
1.	Field for outswing bowler	70
2.	Field for inswing bowler	73
3.	Field for off spin on a good wicket	79
4.	Field for off spin on a turning wicket	80
5.	Field for a slow left-arm bowler on a good wicket	81
6.	Field for a slow left-arm bowler on a turning wicket	81
7.	Field for right-arm leg spin on a good wicket	83
8.	Typical fast bowler's field for a 60-over limited innings	111
9.	Typical slow bowler's field for a 60-over limited innings	112
10.	Typical field for a 40-over limited innings	112

FOREWORD BY

Sir Donald Bradman

One of the happiest moments of my life was the occasion when I opened a letter from Barry Richards' mother.

In it she told me that her son very early in life had read my instruction book *How to Play Cricket* and henceforth had made it his cricketing Bible.

This was a complete surprise because no hint of it had previously reached me. When the work was written I naturally hoped it might influence some youngsters to make cricket their main sport. I was even egotistical enough to think it might be the means of developing some good players. But I had never dreamt it could inspire anyone to become a champion.

I was therefore delighted and gratified beyond words to learn from Barry's mother that his childhood development had in many ways resembled my own. That my career had made such an impact on him.

Later of course I met Barry when he came to South Australia and played a season's first class cricket for my adopted State.

At the risk of making him embarrassed, but believing that his modesty is not likely to be affected by praise, I venture the opinion that no player has ever come to Australia and given us more superb exhibitions of batting.

There were the usual hallmarks of greatness – plenty of time to play his shots, calm and correct footwork, beautiful timing; splendid placing of the ball and a complete range of shots.

I was always thrilled to watch him bat, for here was an artist extracting all those beauties which are inherent in batsmanship, but are so seldom unfolded in full measure.

If only there were enough players of Barry's ability and with his approach to the game there would be no need to think about changing rules or spectator attendance. Regrettably too few have the talent or the dedication to emulate his example.

It naturally follows that I believe Barry is thoroughly qualified to convey to the youth of this and succeeding generations, instructions on how the game should be played.

For me it is a privilege to pay him this tribute. May his book inspire others to follow in his footsteps.

DON BRADMAN.

CHAPTER ONE

Comfort at the Crease

If any young player is going to be a successful batsman, then throughout the season he will be spending hour after hour out there in the middle. I have always believed that this in itself is a good enough reason on its own for making sure that you are comfortable and relaxed at the crease.

Also, if you feel settled with your grip on the bat and your basic stance, it is quite probable that you are on the right road towards a proper technique. The game of cricket has a long history of great batsmen – from stalwarts like the legendary W. G. Grace and the Australian Victor Trumper, down to the Boycotts, Pollocks and Sobers of today. Such players all have individual preferences in style but what they possess in common is a sound technique on which to build their own brand of brilliance.

The way the bat is held – the grip – is fundamental to technique. When I am coaching young boys who have never played the game before I tell them to place their bat on the ground face down and then pick it up as though they were about to chop down a tree. This is the correct grip.

There are two important factors connected with this grip. Firstly, the hands must be close together on the handle. If they are near each other, they will work together. If they are apart, you will find that one is working against the other. This will badly affect the swing of the bat, which will become short and stunted, instead of being the elegant, effective, free-flowing movement that comes from the hands working together.

A common fault in youngsters is a desire to hold the bat too far down the handle in order to obtain more power from their shots. This will, however, only get you into trouble because, in fact, you lose power; the natural swing of the bat is once again stifled.

The classic grip has the top hand – the left hand for right-handed batsmen – pointing out towards cover-point. This is the hand that is all important in so many shots. It guides the stroke and, above all, keeps the ball along the ground. The bottom hand is there to add strength, but it must not dominate, otherwise you will find yourself frequently back in the 'hut' (as county players call the pavilion), out caught. To start with you may find it helpful to grip the bat more firmly with the top hand, and be slightly looser with the other.

Players like Greg Chappell of South Australia who had a spell in England county cricket with Somerset, Ali Bacher, the South Africa Test captain, and John Edrich of Surrey and England, a left-hander, favour a slightly different method. They place the top hand slightly further round the handle towards the back of the bat. If you find that this grip comes naturally to you and you are comfortable using it, then by all means adopt it. Indeed, many Australian players do use it. I find, however, that such a grip does hamper off-side shots, and it becomes that much harder to bring the bat through freely for a shot like the cover drive.

Once you have found a grip with which you feel happy, try not to change it – and remember, whatever shot you are trying to play, never to move your hands around the handle while you are making it. Your grip is, after all, your link with the weapon with which you have to score your runs. It should not be neglected.

A comfortable, evenly balanced stance is equally important as this will enable you to play both back and forward with ease. If you stand with your feet about six inches apart, with your weight evenly spread between the two, you should solve the problem of balance. As a rule of thumb, your feet are roughly in the right position if you can just slide a bat, edge to edge, between them. Position yourself at the wicket with the line of the batting crease bisecting the feet.

I always feel that the best players are those with an upright stance. Try to avoid crouching at the crease. Apart from being extremely uncomfortable, you will find that you tend to topple over. This will disturb the position of the head, especially the eyes, and you will find it very difficult to pick up the line of flight of the ball as it leaves the bowler's hand. Keep your body upright and your head will remain straight and not upset your vision and sense of perspective.

Place the toe of the bat close to, or even just tucked in behind, the back foot. If you hold it away from your body you will find it almost impossible to pick the bat up straight to make your shots; and for a young player a crooked backlift is a short cut to disaster. So pull the bat in close to your body and incline the handle forward so that your hands are resting comfortably against the inside of your front leg.

In my opinion, perhaps the most important part of the body in the stance is the front elbow – the left if you are a right-hander. The left shoulder points towards the bowler, and the elbow is bent ready to guide the top hand, the crucial hand, into action when the ball arrives. By standing in this side-on position, you are perfectly positioned to move either way into the line of each delivery.

Watching first class cricket, you will have noticed that certain players completely flaunt these rules and stand open-chested almost facing the bowler. Perhaps the most famous example of this was Ken Barrington, who scored almost 7,000 runs for England in Test Matches. Why, you might well ask, do I not advocate a method that was so successful at the highest levels of the game? Well, the reason is that Ken, who began his career with an orthodox technique, changed to his front-on style in a shrewd attempt to counter bowlers like the Australian fast left-armer Alan Davidson, who could whip the ball into him through the air and off the seam. It worked, but it did limit the range of Ken's shots. He became a very strong leg-side player, but restricted on the other side of the wicket. For the young player I feel it is too limiting a method, and one which will almost certainly cut your scoring potential by half.

As I have mentioned, how you stand at the wicket will very much determine how you pick up the bat in preparation for each shot you play. Perhaps the golden rule for young batsmen is that they must try to play straight – that is, the bat must swing down vertically into the line of the ball. The logic behind this is simple. With the bat moving vertically to meet the ball, you have a far greater chance of making contact. If the bat is swung horizontally across the line and your timing is not quite right, you will miss and almost certainly begin the long walk back to the pavilion.

To play straight, you must pick the bat up straight. If it goes up crooked it must come down crooked and you will find yourself always playing across the line. The movement comes from the arms and the elbows, not just the wrists, and the bat is taken back in a line towards the stumps. There are two schools of thought on how you should draw the bat back along this imaginary straight line between you and the stumps. One is that the bat's face should be turned open towards point at the top of the swing; you will find that this happens quite naturally as you cock your wrists in lifting the bat. However, my own preference is to take the bat back as it should come down, so that at the top of the swing the face is pointing down at the ground. Both methods will work as long as you keep the backswing straight, so choose whichever of the two you feel more relaxed and comfortable using.

If you have any doubt about your own backswing, go and find yourself a full length mirror. Take up your stance in front of it and pick up the bat. You will soon see whether or not you are tending to play across the line. Whenever I hit a spell of poor form, this is one of the first checks I make. So don't feel self-conscious when you practise in front of a mirror like this; just remember that somewhere there is probably an out-of-form first class batsman doing the very same thing.

How high you should lift the bat does depend to some extent on individual styles and it is difficult to formulate a hard and fast rule. I like to see schoolboys taking the bat back to approximately stump height or perhaps a little higher. Gary Sobers, whose backswing is so smooth, has a backlift that almost carries the bat back into a vertical position, with the handle pointing at the ground. On the other hand Basil D'Oliveira, another free-scoring batsman with a whole range

The grip . . . fundamental to correct batting technique (see Chapter 1)

A rare moment of defence for Essex's Brian 'Tonker' Taylor. Nevertheless, the result is a text-book forward defensive shot (see Chapter 2)

The backward defensive shot. The head is over the line of the ball, the weight is on the back foot, and the top hand is in control, keeping the ball down (see Chapter 2)

Even when there is more aggression in a shot, the bat should come down straight wherever possible (see Chapter 2). The author batting for Hampshire against Lancashire in the 1972 Gillette Cup

The off drive, the classic front-foot attacking shot. Remember, however, that power is not all-important. Runs will only come if the ball is placed wide of the fielders (see Chapter 3)

Never be afraid to go down the wicket and drive the ball over the top. But, like a golfer, do not take your eye off the ball. Otherwise you will be another victim for the wicket-keeper (see Chapter 3)

of attacking shots, hardly seems to lift the bat more than a few inches, using strong wrists to impart power into his strokes. I find it best for my own game to go back around stump high. Again though, what is important is that the blade does come through straight from whatever height you bring it down.

If your back swing is particularly exaggerated, you may find yourself in difficulties against bowlers of genuine pace. Because the bat will take longer to come down, you may become susceptible to the yorker. This delivery, pitching in the block-hole, is aimed at beating your shot at the point which a long backlift will cover last. You will probably get enough of your bat down on a good length ball of particular pace to prevent it getting through, but the full length yorker becomes a tricky proposition.

The way around the problem is to deliberately shorten your backlift when you go out to face a real speed merchant. This method has worked most successfully for me over the years. When I originally came into first class cricket in 1964, South Africa's speed star Peter Pollock was at his peak, and he was very, very quick. I had just left school when I first came up against him in a Currie Cup match, and fortunately I was given this tip of limiting my backlift by the Natal skipper Trevor Goddard. Trevor had learned his lesson on the South African's tour of England in 1955. Then he had faced Frank Tyson who was just back from Australia where his pace bowling had played a huge part in England retaining the African tour of England in 1955. Then he had faced Frank phoon'. By consciously cutting down the time he took to pick up the bat, Trevor had survived most of Tyson's onslaughts.

I have used this method against people like John Snow and Mike Procter and I have made some runs with it. Only use it if you feel that the bowler is a little quick for you, and you will probably find that you can discard it after you have faced a few overs. By then you should have 'got your eye in,' and the fast bowler should be beginning to tire slightly.

With a sound grip, stance, and a naturally straight backlift, you are well on the way towards being ready to go to the wicket with a real prospect of scoring some runs. Because young players, particularly, sometimes lose a little composure when they do go into bat, it is worthwhile just running through a few important preparations you must make before you face your first ball.

The first task is to take guard so that you will always know your bearings in relation to the stumps. When I have been coaching in South Africa and Australia, I have often noticed that a lot of boys come into bat and ask for centre without really knowing why. They just make their mark on the batting crease in line with the centre stump and the wickets at the other end and settle down to bat. But there is an important logic about what guard you should take.

I prefer to take a leg stump guard. I find that from taking up my stance in this position I can tell quite easily whether a delivery has pitched on or off the line between the two stumps; consequently, selecting which shot to play becomes that much easier. I also find that I have plenty of room to play my off-side shots. I think if I took centre as my guard I would find that I did not receive as many balls that I could hit on the off.

Other players prefer to take centre for this very reason. For example, Mike Procter, using a leg stump guard, found that in a series of ten successive dismissals he had been out nine times caught behind the wicket or in the slips. This was because from leg stump he was not getting far enough across to play shots to balls pitching around or outside off stump; the only contact he was making were those little nicks that sent him back to the 'hut'. So he switched to centre, found he had reduced, if not entirely eliminated, the fault and as far as I know he still uses this guard.

There is one other guard that is popular at all levels of cricket, middle and leg or two leg. In this case you make a mark and adopt your stance so that the bat rests in a position covering the middle and leg stumps. I am not an advocate of this guard, because I think it is neither one thing or the other; it falls between two stools. If you have trouble outside the off stump, take centre; if you do not, then take leg stump. From both these positions you are well placed to judge the line of the ball in relation to the stumps.

Whatever guard you use, make a mark that you will be

able to find when you return to that end. Don't rip up the crease, but make a strong enough indentation, either with one of your spikes or the edge of your boot or with the bat itself, that will not disappear under the tramplings of other batsmen. If you do lose your mark, though, don't be afraid to ask for a fresh guard. It will only take a few seconds and it is not worth the risk of making an error of judgement to make a guess at where you should be standing. One final point, always take your guard from the umpire as he stands directly behind the wicket at the other end. Sometimes in school matches, I have seen batsmen asking for guard from where the bowler delivers the ball. This is an unreliable guide and it can only lead to a very rough idea of where the stumps are as you play your shots.

Having taken guard, you will notice that all the good players spend a few seconds looking around the field making a mental note of where each fielder is positioned. As we shall see later in the book, run-making is as much about placement as it is about power. The fielders are placed to stop you scoring runs; if you remember where they are as you play each shot, you will have a much better chance of finding the gaps and keeping your score ticking along. You will also be able to take risks, like hitting the ball in the air, if you know there is no fieldsman in that region waiting to punish any mistake.

So take a good look around you; it will also give you more time to adjust to your surroundings and establish your composure. Then, when you are quite ready, take up your stance. As the bowler runs up you are perfectly prepared to put your batting technique to the test.

CHAPTER TWO

Defensive Technique

As far as I am concerned, technique is all-important in batting. When you are young and your reflexes are at their peak, you may find that you can make runs simply because you have a good eye. But cricket is a game that is enjoyed even at Test level by men in their forties – look at players like Ray Illingworth and Basil D'Oliveira – and at lower levels by men who are even older. Once you reach your later twenties, you are beginning to lose that sharp edge to your reactions and to do well from that point on, you must have a sound technique.

If you do possess this soundness of style, you will also discourage those who bowl at you. Nothing is more heartening to a bowler than to see his opponent leaving a gap between bat and pad, or playing across the line; it gives him real hope of a wicket and something to aim at. If the basics are performed correctly, however, the bowler will begin to wonder if he is wasting his time. The best example in the first class game of a player whose technique breaks bowlers' hearts is Geoff Boycott. You can hardly fit a matchstick between his bat and pad, let alone a cricket ball; most bowlers I know value getting his wicket enormously, particularly if they manage to penetrate his defence and bowl him.

The two prime defensive shots, the forward defensive and the backward defensive, are the pillars of technique. Once you master these two you are certain to stay at the wicket long enough to start playing your attacking strokes. Without them, I think it is fair to say, you will never make a big score

Defensive Technique

against bowling of any quality. Cricket is the worst game in the world if you keep coming back to the pavilion with four or three to your name, but it is a terrific feeling scoring a hundred.

The forward defensive involves, as the name implies, taking a pace forward to meet the ball. Once you have worked on your backlift to make it straight, the rest of the movement follows naturally. Move forward with your front foot to the ball. As soon as you pick up the line of flight, put your foot forward down that line. At the same time, concentrate on remaining sideways on to the bowler, letting your front shoulder, front elbow, and top hand lead you into position. These three parts of the body are crucial to the stroke. Your shoulder must point towards the bowler; if it does not you will find it very difficult to keep your head still and get into line with the path of the ball. Your elbow must be bent and in control; if not you will not be able to keep the bat straight as it swings down into the shot. Your top hand must command the bat; if the bottom hand takes over you will lift the ball and give a catch.

As you move forward, transfer your weight on to the front leg which is bent slightly at the knee. Make sure you do not over-balance and that you keep your back foot on the ground behind the crease. If you play forward and miss to a slow bowler, then topple forward, you will be out stumped. Bring the bat down alongside the pad into the line of the ball and angle the face so that the ball is directed down into the ground; you will find this happens automatically if the top hand is in control. The bottom hand is there simply to support the stroke and keep the bat steady; the forward defensive is a shot you could almost play one-handed.

The crucial point is that there should be no gap between bat and pad; so many players are bowled through this 'gate'. You will be on the way towards eliminating this danger if first you get your foot in line, and second you put your bat in line. It may sound simple but if either is off-line the 'gate' begins to open. In England you will find it safer to make contact with the ball alongside the pad; the ball moves about a lot and if you get an inside-edge from an inswinger, an off-break or cutter you will find that the pad will prevent it flying to short leg or leg slip as a catch. In Australia and South Africa, where there is significantly less movement, you will see more players making contact with their bat in front of the pad. This is one of the ways in which overseas players often find it hard to adapt to English conditions. It is only a minor fault, but without a doubt it is a tighter technique to play with your bat and pad together.

The pad becomes a second line of defence, and, in my mind, it *remains* only a second line of defence. I know a lot of players who, when they first go in, have one main objective, to put the pads in line with the ball and then to wave the bat somewhere near it. They feel that this gives them a sighter. But I am a great believer – and I know Gary Sobers, Graeme Pollock and Mike Procter feel the same – in the use of the bat. After all, that is the object you have been given with which to hit the ball. The pads are there, if you position yourself properly, to help you out if the ball does something unexpected and beats the bat. I have tried never to hit the ball with my pads without trying to first hit it with my bat.

Again, you can begin your practice for the forward defensive in front of a mirror. Go through the movement slowly at first and gradually build up until it becomes natural to you. Then play the shot in front of the mirror to imaginary deliveries pitching from just outside off stump to leg stump. If, in a game, a ball pitches wide of the stumps and there is no chance that it can hit the wicket, you may want to play an attacking stroke to it, but there is no need to play a defensive stroke. It is perfectly safe to allow the ball to pass through to the wicket-keeper.

When you are practising with a ball, ask a friend to stand about eight to ten yards from you and lob the ball underarm on to a good length. Get your front foot into line and play your forward defensive shots. If the weather is bad, you can make do in a gym or a school hall with plastic or tennis balls. Work on the shot for about ten minutes and then let your partner have a turn with the bat.

If the ball drops a little short, it is the backward defensive which is the vital shot that keeps the ball out of the stumps,

Defensive Technique

and this shot deserves as much attention as the forward defensive. Whereas in the forward defensive the first movement is forward, it follows of course that in the backward defensive you take an initial pace back towards your stumps. But in the backward defensive there is another dimension to this first movement; as well as going back it is imperative that you go across. If your foot does not go across, you will not have your head in line with the ball and if your head is not in line your eyes will not be in line.

So as you pick the bat up and you assess the line of flight, move your rear foot back and across into this line. Transfer your weight to this foot and then drag the front foot back until it is almost alongside the other. In doing this, try to ensure that you do not turn square on; hold the side-on position. The front elbow and the top hand again dictate the stroke; keep the elbow bent and hold firmly with the top hand – and you will not cock up a catch for short square leg, or silly mid-on and mid-off.

By going back and across you will be able to cope with any late movement in the air or off the pitch; if your eyes are in line you will be able to adjust should the ball nip back into you or drift away. As with all shots, this will only work if you watch the ball right on to the face of the bat.

If the ball pitches on the leg stump you will have to open up your side-on position slightly because you will have to make contact in front of your body. As long as the eyes are in line and the elbow and top hand direct the ball downwards, it is a simple matter to drop it down in front of you or out on the leg side.

As in the forward defensive, the pads should be used as a second line of defence. As you step across, the back leg should be positioned in line so that if the ball beats the bat or if you get only a little nick, the pads will protect the stumps. Similarly in dragging the front foot back alongside the rear foot you are guarding against the ball that cuts or swings back into you and beats your intended shot.

As in the forward defensive you are looking to play the backward defensive to deliveries pitching on the stumps or those that pitch outside the stumps but might be moving in on target. If the ball is wide you may as well leave it alone as play a defensive shot. Early in an innings you can cultivate the art of letting a swinging delivery pass safely through to the keeper. Bowlers like the Australian Test quickies Dennis Lillee and Graham McKenzie, or the Surrey and England paceman Geoff Arnold, run the ball away from the bat both through the air and off the seam. If you go back and across so that you are covering middle and off and the ball is still outside your line, you can be almost certain that the natural swing will carry the ball wide of the stumps. So you can safely let it pass, whereas if you play at it you might well edge the ball to the keeper or the slips. I found when I came out of school, that I used to play at these types of delivery and I used to get out in this way, so I learned the hard way about letting the ball go. One of the best leavers of a ball in first class cricket was Bill Lawry of Australia; he seemed to be able to calculate each ball to minute fractions. He got into such a position that he could withdraw his bat at the very last minute. On the Australian tour of South Africa in 1970, Mike Procter tried to upset Lawry by going round the wicket at him and altering the angle of flight, and this did make him think twice about letting certain deliveries go. One of the qualities that one should demand from bowlers is that they make batsmen play at their deliveries, particularly early in the innings, and it can be infuriating to the chap bowling at you if you safely let pass balls that he might have expected you to play at. Apart from the fact that you are getting a sighter, you may find that leaving the ball will give you a psychological 'edge' over the bowler.

You will find that you can only do this, however, when you are adopting the correct backward defensive position. So practise in front of the mirror again and then go out on to the grass or into the gym and get a friend to lob the ball from about ten yards on to a spot about ten feet in front of you; this will force you to go back. Remember above all that it is back and ACROSS.

One of the great problems in batting is to decide whether to play back or forward. Obviously the well-pitched-up delivery should be met by a forward stroke, whereas the short ball should send you on to the back foot, but in between there are all sorts of deliveries pitching on a variety of lengths about which a decision has to be made.

The answer is more a matter of physique and style than a hard and fast rule. In terms of physique, obviously if you are a tall fellow with long legs you can step further forward than a short chap. If you are around the six foot mark, I think it most advisable to use the full length of your reach and to play forward as often as you can. Players like Graeme Pollock – who is a couple of inches over six foot – will get on to the front foot wherever possible; in fact Graeme only ever gets on to the back foot to pull or cut really short deliveries. To play a backward defensive he really does little more than move across and stand up to his full height; there is really no need for him to move too far back.

Don Bradman was, perhaps, the best example of how a diminutive man selects whether to go forward or back. He rarely played forward, because his reach was so insubstantial. He looked to get on to the back foot and consequently scored a lot more runs with hooks and cuts than a man of average height. By watching the ball closely, and keeping his head over the line, he was able to step back to balls relatively full in length and still cope with any late movement.

As you play more and more cricket and increase your experience, you will soon judge whether you are a back-foot player or a front-foot player, according to what suits you best. Almost every player comes into one of these two categories. Often your height will dictate this, but if you are reasonably tall but still like to play back, continue to do so – providing of course you are making runs regularly with this method!

The conditions and the quality of the pitches you play on will probably influence your choice. I think there are more front players in England than there are in the hotter countries. Again, this is because there is less movement for the bowlers on the baked-hard pitches of Australia and South Africa; there you can go back to almost anything knowing that if you get in line your bat will not be beaten by the ball deviating off the wicket. In England, where softer pitches, that are regularly soaked in rain, enable the ball to bite into the surface and shoot off at an angle, there is plenty to learn from the old dictum 'when in doubt push out'. In playing forward you are moving nearer to the pitch of the ball and stand a better chance of covering any movement. If ever the ball comes back into you it will strike the pads if you have played the shot correctly. Since in playing forward your front leg is well down the wicket, it is unlikely that you will be given out l.b.w.

One way to judge if you are a front or back player is whether your first movement when the ball is released is forward or to the rear. Particularly against the quicker bowlers almost every batsman starts to go one way before checking back if the length of the ball makes such a shot inadvisable. I do not think I know of any top-class batsman who stands completely still as a fast bowler delivers the ball. I used to think that Tom Graveney might do so, but even he made a move, and a strange one at that. When I came over to England with Mike Procter in 1965 and spent a year on the Gloucestershire staff, it was one of my great ambitions to see Graveney bat. He had left the county by then and was playing for Worcestershire, but I finally got my wish when they came to Cheltenham to play Gloucestershire.

Being a great fan of his, I scrutinised every ball he faced, and I spotted this strange movement. His first reaction was most unclassic when you consider how stylish he was in every other respect; he moved his right leg back about six inches, away towards square leg! Then he played forward, and to all intents and purposes he was a front foot player, but he did make this little movement backwards first.

Against spin bowlers I find it perfectly possible to remain still until I have judged where the ball is going to pitch. However, against the speed men I do make a move; I go back and across. Across is once more the vital thing; by going across you are getting yourself in line with the spot from which they deliver the ball. John Snow, Dennis Lillee and Mike Procter, probably the world's three quickest bowlers, are hurling the ball at you at around 75 m.p.h., so there is not much time for it to swing about. Once I am in this position, I find that I rarely have to adjust to any great extent to hit the ball. In going back you do have an extra yard in which to see the ball; that may not sound a lot, but against bowlers of such pace it can make that little bit of difference.

All this is a matter of style rather than technique. Once you have acquired the technique of these two basic defensive shots, you will develop your own style of play. Until you acquire them, then no matter what style you adopt you will find it very difficult to stay at the crease for any length of time.

But once you have mastered these two strokes, you are likely to survive the tricky first few balls that you have to face. You will be set, with your eye in, all ready to attack. . . .

CHAPTER THREE

Attack off the Front Foot

For me the great enjoyment of batting comes when I am on the attack. Obviously there are times when you have to defend, when the interests of the team dictate that you must survive – but cricket is all about scoring runs and to score runs at a reasonable speed you must be able to attack. I am not talking about slogging or about taking stupid risks. Attacking play means using legitimate scoring shots to build up your own and your side's total. If you allow the bowler to dominate he will bowl all the better; but if he knows that you will hit the ball for four and be looking to score off any delivery that is slightly off line, he will never feel totally in command.

When you are attacking off the front foot, the basic shot is the drive. Whether the drive sends the ball sweetly through the covers, firmly back past the bowler or whistling wide of mid-on, it is one of the most exhilarating shots in the game. Played correctly it can give immense satisfaction not only to the batsman but also to the spectators, because it is such a beautifully flowing stroke. When people talk about batting being an art this is the type of shot that inspires them.

The ideal delivery to drive off the front foot is the half volley or a low full toss. If you can trust the bounce of the pitches on which you play, you can widen the scope of this shot by driving 'on the up'; that is to play the stroke to a good length delivery. On the hard wickets of South Africa and Australia where the ball comes through true, I have found hitting the ball 'on the up' relatively safe and certainly very lucrative. In England, with so much more movement about, the shot has sometimes got me out – either by mistiming to give a catch in the covers or by edging to slip. It really is not a shot to be recommended until you have a few runs under your belt or if the side needs a quick score. So stick to the half volleys and full tosses to begin with, until you have mastered the technique.

Whether you are driving on the off side, the leg side or straight, the basics of the technique are the same, although where you place each shot will depend on the line of that particular delivery. I always think of the drive as a continuation of the forward defensive shot, but with one important exception. The ball should always be met level with the front foot; never in front of it.

Again there is a crucial link with your backlift, and the time you have spent improving it will prove invaluable as you look to develop the drive. The bat must come down clean and straight as you begin the shot. As soon as you have made up your mind to drive a particular delivery, move your front foot forward so that the toe goes to the pitch of the ball – just as you would do for the forward defensive. What this does *not* mean is actually putting your foot where the ball will drop; this is a common fault and one that can be painful in several ways.

I remember playing one of my first games at a very early age at school, and falling into this trap when I was looking to play a straight drive to a ball on the stumps. I got my foot so close to the pitch of the ball that it literally landed on my big toe, and I could not get my bat to it because my foot got in the way. To cap it all I was given out l.b.w. and I had to limp back to the pavilion. I quickly learned my lesson.

I must, however, continually emphasise that it is equally important not to be more than three or four inches away, or that 'gate' will open up. After the ball has disappeared through that, you will quickly be disappearing from the crease.

Like the forward defensive, the drive is a side-on shot. As you move forward, transferring the weight on to the front leg, you are all the time showing the bowler the left side of your body if you are a right-hander or the right side if you are a left-hander. Again, keep the front elbow as high as possible, allowing the top hand to control the shot and keep the ball along the floor.

Although there is a vast difference in technique between the golfer's swing and the batsman's flowing movement into the drive, there is one crucial similarity. If the golfer takes his eye off the ball and lifts his head the chances are that he will hit thin air and that the ball will still be sitting on the tee when he has finished his swing. Cricketers fall into the same trap, only the ball will not be sitting still, it will be on its way to disturbing the stumps. So watch the ball right on to the face of your bat and never lift your head. The tendency is to look where you expect the ball to go before you actually make contact. If you do throw your head up in the air the chances are you will not dispatch the ball anywhere at all.

The power in the shot comes from a full swing of the arms, beginning with the backlift and ending with a strong follow-through. When you are learning the drive, the follow-through is sometimes a problem. Most players follow-through so that the bat goes right over their shoulder; the one notable exception in first-class cricket whom I have seen is Colin Cowdrey. He checks his follow-through as soon as the bat is in a horizontal position. For youngsters I think Cowdrey's method has much to commend it; it really ensures that you play the shot correctly, keeping the bat straight down and through the line of the ball. So often youngsters want to knock the cover off the ball and knowing that the drive does permit them an extravagant follow-through, they launch themselves avidly into the shot. The result is rarely a perfect off-drive; more often the bottom hand is allowed to take charge, the bat is swung across the line and a horrible cow shot is the result. If you have the opportunity, watch Cowdrey bat and see how technically correct this method allows him to be. Of course, once you play the shot naturally with a straight bat you can allow yourself the full follow-through, but always take care not to let it dominate.

Extra power can be added from the wrists, but again you

Attack off the Front Foot

must beware of letting that bottom hand take control of the shot. If you allow it to whip through, you will be back to the inelegant, ineffective cow shot.

Balance is another key to the success of the drive. You will find it much easier to remain in a balanced position, as well as finding it easier to watch the ball, if you keep your head still when you play the shot. Try to keep your left ear (or your right if you are a left-hander) touching your leading shoulder; this should keep your head still. Again, the bottom hand can be so disruptive; if it pulls through your head will fall over to the off side and your eyes will not be looking at the ball along a level plane. This in turn can lead to complete over-balance, and if you are toppling over to the off side as you play your shot you will never time it properly.

If you do over-balance, your back foot, which as in the forward defensive is resting as a prop behind the batting crease, may come up; if you miss the ball you are at the mercy of an alert wicket-keeper.

As I have said, the line of the ball almost always determines the part of the ground to which you are going to play your drive. If the ball pitches outside the off stump the target will be the boundary rope through the covers; if it pitches around off stump you will be looking to hit it through mid-off, or if it pitches leg stump the ball is dispatched through mid-on. The only real exceptions are when your side needs runs quickly and you have to improvise by, for example, hitting across the line to get the ball away on the leg side, or by backing away to leg to make space to hit a ball that pitches leg stump, away through a gap on the off side. You will often see batsmen playing this way in limited-over cricket, like the John Player League in England. But it is a measure for emergencies only. Generally the rule is the wider the ball is outside the off stump the squarer your off-drive will be; the nearer the stumps the straighter it will be.

You should follow this basic guide until you have totally mastered the techniques of the drive. The position of your toes on the front foot should determine the direction of your drive; they should always point in the direction you are aiming to strike the ball. Thus in the cover drive the front foot should be placed almost square on to the bowler.

The on-drive has its own particular problems. Many young players in playing the stroke put their whole leg in line with the ball instead of just the toe of the front. If this happens, the drive is played around the pads and the ball will be dragged around square on the leg-side rather than struck wide of mid-on. One reason this occurs is the tendency to move forward along the line of around middle stump. If the ball is on line with leg stump it becomes very difficult to adjust quickly and reposition the front leg further to the leg-side.

The more the on-drive is played across the front leg, the less the chance that you will middle the ball and the greater the risk of it flying up in the air. Try this for yourself in front of the mirror. If you are straining to reach the ball in front of your pads, you will see how you begin to topple over on the off-side. As this happens, the face of the bat meets the ball not directing it into the ground but angled upwards.

This is a problem that does not only occur among youngsters; top-class batsmen experience the same difficulties. Perhaps the best example is Arthur Short who plays with me for Natal. He is a good enough player to have been selected for the 1970 tour of England and the 1971-72 tour of Australia, both of which were unfortunately cancelled, but he has had real problems playing the on-drive. He has been out many times caught in the mid-wicket area, because he does fall into this trap. He stretches his front leg too far across, has to reach around his pad to get to the ball and the result is often a little chip into the fielder's hands.

Graham Roope, one of the most promising of England's new generation of batsmen, went through a very bad spell at the start of the 1971 season in just the same way. A front-foot player, Roope moved into position just a little too early and, like Arthur Short, played across his front leg. If you find yourself in this position playing the on-drive, the safest way to try to extricate yourself is to go through with the shot. If you feel just before you make contact that you are off balance and that the ball is going to go in the air, try to clear the fielder. If you check the shot, the likely result is that you will spoon a little dolly catch. If you really hit the ball in the middle of the bat, you may well see the ball bouncing over the ropes. However, this is no justification for playing the shot in this way; it will get you out as often as it brings you boundaries.

With so many inswing and off-spin bowlers bringing the ball into you, the on-drive played with the correct technique can be an extremely lucrative stroke. Do not neglect it. Quite probably it will not come naturally, but don't be dismayed. Practice may not make you perfect, but it certainly can turn you into an efficient on-driver.

There is one golden rule in run-making that applies to all attacking shots, but particularly to the drive. Although the stroke must be well-timed, it is not how hard you hit the ball but where you hit it that matters. Most youngsters love to give the ball a good whack – and I was no exception when I was at school – but an obsession with brute force can get you out and, if you think carefully about it, actually cut down the number of runs you make. The secret of gathering runs is placement rather than power.

Most fielders, fielding correctly, will stop a hard shot struck directly at them, but they will find it considerably more difficult to cut down your flow of runs if you place a shot of less power wide of them. Then they have to turn and chase. You get the runs whilst gradually the fielder becomes tired and more liable to make a mistake. Try to keep a picture in your mind of where the fielders are placed when you are taking strike and consciously steer your shots into the gaps between them.

If you have ever seen my fellow countryman Graeme Pollock bat, you will know just what I mean. I think Graeme is one of the best post-War batsmen in the world; he scores an incredible proportion of his runs in boundaries. Obviously he is a big, powerful chap, but those fours come because the ball is driven into the spaces available to him. I still love to hit the ball hard, but as a professional batsman it is my job to score as many runs as I can, and I assure you that even when I do hit the ball hard I am always trying to strike it through a gap in the field.

Of course, when you are playing the drive, there is an alternative method you can employ to beat the field – that is, to loft the ball over the fielders. I am a great believer in hitting over the top, provided you play the shot with a fluent, straight swing. For me the perfect lofted drive flies back over the bowler's head or, at its widest, over mid-on or mid-off. The shot itself is a simple and natural extension of the drive that keeps the ball on the ground except that the bottom hand plays a more critical role. The toe goes as near to the pitch as possible, the bat swings through straight and then on contact the bottom hand comes through and boosts the normal swing. Be very careful not to let the bottom hand take control of the complete swing otherwise you will play across the line; and remember to watch the ball right on to the bat. If your concentration lapses slightly you will find your head will go up too soon and over will go the stumps.

Hitting over the top must be spontaneous. So many players seem to think, if they have blocked three balls and are wondering how they are going to score, that a belt over the fielders is the answer. It just doesn't work that way. It has to be an instantaneous reaction – you are looking to drive, you find that the ball is not quite far enough up, but you decide to go through with the shot by simply swinging the bat smoothly through the line. It is not a slog, just this complete, balanced swing. Some of the hugest sixes come when the batsman has just followed right through, almost effortlessly, and allowed the timing to carry the ball over the ropes. In the same way, so often you will see a player really wind himself up for the big hit over the top and then hole out at mid-on, just because he has been obsessed by using brute force in the shot. With timing, the drive over the top will always carry for six.

Often, when someone like Alan Knott lofts the ball to the boundary, you will see how he uses his feet to skip down the wicket to get to the pitch of the ball. This is an art in itself and if you spend the time learning how to do it properly you will widen the range of your attacking shots. By

Attack off the Front Foot

coming down the track, you can turn good length deliveries into half volleys and full tosses, and the ball you might otherwise have been happy to block you can now score from. Also, if the ball is turning, quick footwork will take you down to the pitch of the ball where the spin can most effectively be countered.

Until you are an experienced player, restrict yourself to coming out to slow bowlers. In county cricket the Lancashire and India wicket-keeper/batsman, Farookh Engineer, makes quite a habit of 'charging' the faster bowlers. Just look at it from the bowler's viewpoint. He bowls what he thinks is a good length ball only to find that Farookh has turned it into a half volley and smacked it for four. What does he bowl next? Another good length delivery? The same quick footwork might turn it into another boundary. Drop it shorter then? Well, if Farookh stays his ground, then he is likely to hook or pull a short length ball. Pitch it up further, perhaps? Then it might become a straight half volley and still be struck to the fence. . . ! You see the problem and the advantage of coming down the wicket. The batsman *must* dictate to the bowler to stay on top, and once you have got him wondering where to bowl he is almost certainly going to give you some loose ones to score off. Farookh is an exception, but to slow spinners copy his example. Bowlers love to wheel away at players who seem to be chained to the crease; these batsmen are always being dictated to, rather than assuming command.

Of course with the wicket-keeper standing up, missing the ball will mean almost certain dismissal, so you must master the right style of footwork. Otherwise it will be the bowler who has the last laugh. You must think of the movement as a glide down the track – not a jump, a lunge or a rush. To focus perfectly on the ball your eyes must stay on the same plane all the time you are moving out; if your head goes up or down, your sense of perspective will be disturbed and you will find it that much harder to gauge where the ball is going to bounce.

Move out sideways. Keep that front shoulder pointing at the bowler. Take the first pace with the front foot then move up the back foot until it is actually in front of the front foot, then move off with the front foot again. By now you should have reached the pitch of the ball, but if you are a short fellow you may find you need to repeat the move once more.

I have always stuck to one rule when going down the wicket. Go all the way and do not be indecisive. If you find that you are not quite in position to play an attacking shot when you have given the bowler the 'charge', you can always simply relax into a forward defensive shot and block the ball. If you know you are not going quite to get there and you decide instead to try to come back and fend the ball away, you will find yourself in terrible trouble. So be positive. I always feel that it is better to be stumped by a yard or two than by a matter of inches. The result is the same, but at least you have got out trying to attack.

Go back in front of your mirror to begin your practice for the drive. The points to check particularly are that your head and eyes are kept still as you go through with the shot. Work particularly on the on-drive position, so that it becomes a natural movement for you to take that front step down the line of leg stump; from there you will be able to lean easily into the shot.

And whenever you have the opportunity, pop along to the nearest first-class cricket match to your home and watch how the top-class players perform the shot. It will help you get the feel of how and when the stroke is played.

But the basic practice must involve a ball – and to begin with, a tennis ball. Ask a friend to stand a pace or two in front of you and about two feet to the off-side of your stance. He drops the ball so that it lands in front of you, and you must move forward to drive it on the half volley as it bounces for a second time. This routine is excellent practice for all the drives and it has the added advantage of providing fielding practice for a large number of boys positioned in an arc from mid-wicket to cover-point.

From this you can graduate to net practice with a cricket ball. Begin gently by asking your friend to serve to you again. This time he can throw the ball from about ten yards, concentrating on keeping it up to you so that you can play the drive. Then as you develop the feel for the shot and the confidence in your own ability, you can move on to a full-scale net practice, with the bowlers again under instruction to bowl a full length so that you have the maximum opportunity to sharpen your new weapon.

Never neglect the drive. I have always regarded the stroke as one of the most important in my own game. Not only has it been an important source of runs, but it has also enabled me to obtain that vital psychological boost over bowlers. As a breed, none of them like to be hit, but what is especially disconcerting to them is to see a delivery driven effortlessly back past them to the boundary. Whether it is John Snow in a Test Match or the local 'quickie' in village cricket, the bowler tends to become a little disturbed. And if you can upset the bowler you are halfway towards making a big score.

Of course the drive is not the only scoring shot that can be played off the front foot; runs can be gathered from pushes and deflections as well as from the more firmly struck strokes.

When watching first-class cricket you have probably noticed how often batsmen collect singles and twos from what appear to be no more than nudges of the bat, particularly on the leg-side. In the game we call this 'working the ball away' and almost every county side has its quota of 'workers'; at Hampshire our all-rounder, Peter Sainsbury, lives off this shot, and Mike Smith the former England captain who plays for Warwickshire, is perhaps the best in the world.

Much of their leg-side efficiency comes from being able to play the leg glance, off both front and back feet. The glance off the front foot is particularly effective off a quick bowler because you can use the pace of his delivery to send the ball off an angled bat down to fine leg.

The secret of the shot is to time the moment when you angle the face of the bat. There is not much margin for error; if you turn the face too soon, the ball will hit the back of the bat and probably lob up for a simple caught-and-bowled; if you turn too late, you will not make any contact at all. The aim is to make contact just as the ball arrives level with your front foot on a line with leg stump or just outside. It is very risky to attempt the glance to anything pitching on middle and leg, middle or off stumps; if you miss, there is bound to be a heck of a shout for l.b.w.

As you turn the face, drop your wrists so that not only is the bat angled but it is angled downwards; the glance is a controlled deflection, not just an inside edge, and you must make sure that you are not cocking up a catch straight to leg slip. As with every other shot we have discussed, the top hand is so important. If you let the top hand lead you through the glance, the ball will be safely directed into the ground; if the bottom hand pushes through, leg slip will always fancy his chances of ending your innings.

The glance is often referred to as the leg tickle and that is really an apt description of the shot. The ball is played very late, at almost the last possible moment, and very gently angled away from around the leg stump. As I have said, the pace mostly comes from the velocity with which the ball is bowled, although by whipping the wrists into the stroke you will be able to add power. Beware of this though, because as soon as you are looking for more force, it is the fatal bottom hand that comes into the shot. Power is no good to you if it lifts the ball into a fielder's hands.

The ball can also be glanced on the off-side, off the front foot, down to third man, but this is a much more risky shot. I mention it because top-class players do use it and before you attempt to copy it, it is worth pointing out the risks. This shot is often referred to as 'opening the face' because that is really what happens. In pushing forward around the off-stump the bat is angled to the off-side instead of going through firmly facing the bowler as in the orthodox forward defensive. As a result the ball is deflected down to third man.

The danger comes when you are not quite in line or the ball moves about a little. Usually medium or fast bowlers have two slips and a gully waiting for a snick, and if the face is not opened at precisely the right moment and you get a 'nick' there are expert catchers ready to gobble up the chance. Because of the rule that permits only two fielders behind the wicket on the leg side, there can only be two leg slips; in fact there is rarely more than one because the other fielder is usually set back on the long-leg boundary to stop the four. The leg glance is therefore considerably safer, and only a very poorly executed shot is going to send you back to the 'hut'.

So avoid opening the face, even if you are a Surrey fan and have spent a lot of time watching Micky Stewart hoarding runs with little nudges down to third man; that is his speciality and he has been a top-class player for over twenty years. It is not something that you can copy overnight.

The other major attacking shot off the front foot is the sweep, and for the first time we are talking about making contact with a cross-bat. This is an effective shot, particularly on a turning wicket when you are using the spin that brings the ball into you. Although I am basically a straight player, I do play the sweep and I have scored a lot of runs with it. But I do have some reservations.

All cross-batted shots have a degree of risk about them, because you are swinging the bat across the line rather than down and through it. I think you should reserve the sweep for when you are playing well and you have a few runs under your belt. It really is not the sort of shot to play in your first few overs; the chances of mistiming are strong.

The classic sweep begins by putting your toe as near as possible to the pitch of the ball. You then swing the bat horizontally across the front of your leg, aiming to hit it away square on the leg side. As you make contact, roll the wrists over so that the ball is played down into the ground. You can play the sweep to any pitched-up delivery that is going to go wide of the leg stump, because you know that if you miss you are not going to be out l.b.w.

Funnily enough, the ideal ball to sweep is one that pitches outside the off stump when you are facing an off-spinner on a turning wicket. You can hit across the line safely knowing that because your leg is now outside the line between the two stumps you cannot be l.b.w.

Basil D'Oliveira and Colin Cowdrey are, perhaps, the two best known players who adopt a different sweeping technique. Instead of playing the shot in front of their left legs they wait until the ball has passed and is moving down the leg-side. Then they play it down towards fine-leg, rather than square, with a stroke that almost resembles a tennis smash with the bat pointing to the sky. It is more lucrative than the normal sweep because so often the fielder on the boundary is too square to cut it off but it is very hard to master unless you have done it naturally since you were very young.

The sweep is a stroke you will find that you are using more as you improve as a player. I really do not recommend it when you are finding your feet at the crease. Concentrate on playing straight to start with. If later you find that you want to sweep, spend some time practising it in the nets until you are happy with your technique. Then give it a go when an opportunity presents itself in a match. After that, results will tell you whether it is suitable for you or not.

With a range of front foot shots at your disposal, you are halfway towards becoming the attacking cricketer. But what happens when the bowler begins to pitch short of a length...?

CHAPTER FOUR

Attack off the Back Foot

Like aggressive front play, attack off the back foot is a combination of shots played with the bat vertical and horizontal. The force off the back foot and the leg glance are played with the bat coming through straight, whereas the hook, the pull and the cut are all shots in which the ball is struck cross-batted. Yet in all these shots the initial movement is the same; the rear foot goes back towards the stumps and across towards the off-side. If you have mastered your back defensive play, you will be in a perfect position to extend the range of your back-foot shots into run-getting strokes.

Of all these shots, the forcing stroke off the back foot is perhaps the hardest. But because in making the shot the bat remains straight and you hit through the line rather than across it, I am a great believer in making use of it. As I have said before, you have a much better chance of adjusting the stroke if the ball moves, or of getting away with an error of judgement, if the bat comes through straight.

Just how straight you can keep your bat in this shot largely depends on how tall you are. The big fellows like Graeme Pollock or the Sussex and England all-rounder Tony Greig have a tremendous advantage because they can swing the bat through perfectly straight and still get over the top of the ball to direct it down into the ground. This shot is particularly closely linked to the backward defensive; you go back and across to get in line and then, because the delivery is particularly short, you are looking to do more than just drop the ball down in front of you. If it is around off-stump you are looking to crack it away through the covers or if it has pitched about leg-stick you will strike it through mid-on.

The danger, especially if you are on the short side, is that the bottom hand will be used to power the ball away; if this is so, the chances are that the face of the bat will be pointing upwards on contact with the ball and that mid-off or mid-on is going to get a catch. Unless you are a six-footer who can lean powerfully into the shot and direct the ball downwards, there are two alternatives, either of which should prevent you continually holing out when forcing off the back foot.

One way is to pull yourself up to your full height by standing right up on your toes so that when the ball arrives you are right on top of it. The problem in doing this is maintaining balance. Obviously you have to be perfectly in position when up on your toes because if you then find you have to adjust, the chances are that you will topple over. Anything that causes your eyes or head to be disturbed from focusing on the ball will endanger the success of the shot.

However, if you do move back and across and the ball is sufficiently short to be forced, go up on those toes, bring the bat down straight and you should find that you have sufficient height to play the ball downwards. If you suddenly realise that you are not going to be able to keep it down, check the shot and settle for a backward defensive stroke with a dead bat.

But perhaps a more common way of dealing with the awkwardness of forcing off the back foot is to compromise on the straightness of the bat. Many players, including myself, find it profitable to bring the bat down at an angle around halfway between horizontal and vertical. This does enable you to combat the difficulty of hitting the ball into the ground, because you are allowing yourself a better chance of lifting the bat higher. Just try it for yourself; pick up a bat and aim for an imaginary ball bouncing about waist height. It is awkward, isn't it, to make contact with the middle of the bat if you are keeping the bat vertical? Once you allow yourself to incline it towards the horizontal, the easier the movement and the greater the power you feel you can impart.

Attack off the Back Foot

But in performing this very simple exercise, you can see immediately the drawbacks of playing with a more horizontal bat. Your head is automatically withdrawn from the line of flight and your eyes are off line; you are playing the ball further away from your body. In fact, rather than leaning into the shot, you are pulling away from it to give yourself room to bring through this angled bat.

I find that I play the shot this way, particularly against left-arm spinners who are turning the ball away from me. I can lean back and strike the ball with the bat angled at about 45 degrees, hitting it probably between cover and extra cover. But there is undoubtedly a certain amount of risk attached to adopting this technique, and if I can come through with a straight bat to punch the ball away I'll try my hardest to do so. As I am sure you have appreciated already in this book, I am a great preacher of the virtues of the straight bat, in the force off the back foot as much as in any shot. But sometimes for no other reason than the way you are built you have to compromise and if the compromise works for you then don't become too tied to the text book.

The straight bat can also be used to deflect the ball behind the wicket off the back foot, particularly on the leg side. The dangers of going on to the back foot and deflecting the ball down to third man with a twist of the face of a straight bat are exactly the same as those we discovered when examining this shot off the front foot. Professionals may have this shot practised to a fine art, but I am sure very few of them would recommend it to a young player. Just the slightest miscalculation and the wicket-keeper, the slips and the gully will be waiting to pounce; and because you are not actually imparting any power into the shot, rather using the bowler's own pace, the chances are that any catch you do give will not be travelling at great speed.

The leg glance off the back foot is an altogether more genuine shot. It should be played to a short delivery pitching around leg stump, and the ball should be turned away off your hip. As you move back and across, the ball is bouncing up towards what was your front hip in the stance, and at the very last moment before it strikes your body you angle the ball down towards fine leg. Once more the top hand controls the shot to direct the ball into the ground. This is even more important than in the glance off the front foot, because the short ball is lifting that much higher. If you do not get over the ball, leg slip will be fancying his chances of putting an end to your stay at the crease.

Once you have eliminated any danger of the top hand being overruled by its partner – and you can do this in the nets – the only major risk in this shot occurs if you play the ball too far away from your body. In other words, instead of flicking it away off your hip, you are making contact six inches away from your legs. Again, just pick up your bat and play the shot this way in front of your mirror and you will immediately see why you lessen the odds of scoring runs and increase your chances of getting out. Your eyes are no longer in line with the ball and the delicate timing of the angling of the bat in the glance becomes a very difficult proposition.

Because my initial movement is back and across, once or twice in my career I have found that I have gone too far towards the off stump in playing the glance. The result has been that I have had to reach for the ball away from my legs and I have only made faint contact and given the keeper a straightforward leg-side catch. If your hip is directly behind the bat and you only get a little tickle on the ball, then you will not be caught behind because your body will prevent the deflection going anywhere near the keeper.

That extra fraction of a second that you have to see the ball when you play off the back foot does give you time to increase the range of your attacking shots, particularly allowing you to position yourself to hit across the line of flight.

The hook shot is, perhaps, the most thrilling of these strokes as the batsman twists himself into a really fast delivery and cracks it to the fence. Above all, it is a brave shot and a most effective weapon against the speed merchant who likes to threaten the batsman by pitching the ball short of a length and bouncing it up at his chest.

Basically I think the hook is an instinctive shot and you

will know in yourself whether you want to hook or whether you will settle for the alternative of ducking under or swaying out of the way of the bouncer. It is very hard, although possible, to turn yourself into a hooker if you don't possess this natural inclination to play the shot; equally if you do find the shot comes automatically to you, you will find it very hard to resist.

The ideal delivery to hook is the ball that bounces about head high or a fraction higher. You move back and across, transferring your weight on to the back foot, and, pivoting on this foot, you swing the bat across the line of flight. On contact the wrists must be rolled over so that the ball is struck downwards. If you are a proficient hooker, you will find that an astute quick bowler will try to bounce the ball above your head so that it becomes impossible for you to turn your wrists over the top of the shot. If you middle the shot you may find the crowd applauding a six, but they might have a catch at deep square leg to cheer instead; you are just as likely not to middle it, probably sending up a skier or just getting a little nick to the keeper. The moral is clear – if the ball bounces high, try your hardest to resist the temptation.

Keith Stackpole is the best hooker I have ever seen. He is so much in control of the shot that he not only hits the ball into the ground he hits it in front of square – a terrific testimony to how quickly he gets into the correct position. In the 1972 series between England and Australia, Stackpole set a wonderful example, especially to his own teammates. Most Australians like to hook because the ball does bounce in their own country, but some tend to hook off balance or without rolling their wrists over. The touring party could not have had a better lesson than to watch their own vice-captain in action.

I enjoy playing the hook shot, because to me it is an instinctive reaction to a bumper. But what really makes me believe that this shot cannot be premeditated is a scar that I have just above my left eye. I was playing in a none-too-serious single-wicket competition in South Africa and my opponent was Peter Pollock. For the enjoyment of the crowd we had an agreement that he would drop one short and I would try to hook it for six. So he duly came rushing up to the wicket, and bowled the bouncer, but I was in position far too early, got myself in a terrible tangle and took the blow on the forehead. I am sure that if I had not known the bouncer was coming I would have reacted in a much more instinctive way and played the shot successfully.

The only other time I have been hit hooking was on a very slow wicket when I went to clobber Mike Procter to the ropes, but I had completed the shot before the ball arrived. Fortunately the damage was only slight.

If you find that you are always hit on the gloves hooking or that the shot does frequently cause your dismissal, then you have an alternative. Either cut it out completely or go back to the nets to sort the shot out. This is, after all, what practice is all about; grab hold of a friend and tell him to come and bounce balls at you until you have worked out what is wrong and ironed it out.

To make the practice even more realistic, find yourself a piece of smooth concrete and ask your friend to bounce a cork, composition ball at you. This will really fly up at you from the solid surface, but in a true way so that the physical danger is minimal if you play the shot correctly. After their problems with John Snow's bouncers in the 1970-71 Australia-England series, Greg and Ian Chappell practised in this way before the 1972 tour. Both looked vastly more confident against Snow's exceptional pace, although Ian's tendency to hook upwards cost him his wicket on a couple of occasions.

In schoolboy cricket, however, opportunities to use the hook shot are much rarer because few young bowlers have the strength to make the ball bounce head high. More often the ball pitched short comes up around waist height and the shot to play to this type of delivery is the pull rather than the hook. There are many similarities between the pull and the hook; you go back and across into the line of flight, you swing the bat horizontally across the ball's path and you roll the wrists over as you play the shot so that it does not fly up in the air. But instead of aiming square or behind the square-leg umpire, in the pull you are looking to hit the ball in front of the wicket, either between mid-on and mid-wicket or between mid-wicket and square-leg.

The pull is perhaps the most natural of all shots, because it comes from an instinctive swing of the arms; it is the sort of swing you would use to chop down a tree or even to throw a ball. The arms come across the front of the body. What is peculiar about the shot is that it is the only one I know in which you start with your weight on one foot and end up with it transferred to the other. You step back because the ball is short and your weight is now on the back foot; your front leg is placed outside the line of the stumps and as you swing the bat through and across in front of you, your weight almost exactly follows this path. By the time you have completed your follow-through all the weight ends up on the front leg. In making this movement what in effect you are doing is putting all your body into the stroke. Most shots rely on timing for the power; as we have already seen, if you try to throw your whole weight behind the cover drive, for example, you are likely to destroy the necessary rhythm of stroke-play. But in the pull you can put everything behind the shot. I am sure if you threw up a cricket ball to anyone and asked them to whack it as hard as they could they would use the pull shot.

But do remember to pull downwards; however hard you crack the ball a safe catcher at mid-on or mid-wicket will hang on to the chance if it comes at a catchable height. If you have any trouble with the shot, put yourself in front of that mirror and check that you are turning your wrists correctly. As you start the pull the back of your top hand and the clenched fingers of your bottom hand should be facing upwards. At the end of the shot, the positions should be reversed – the back of your bottom hand and the fingers of your top hand should be pointing to the sky.

Although I never saw him play live, Don Bradman must have been the greatest puller of all time. From the film clips I have seen of his many memorable innings, this one shot stood out time and time again. Probably because he was such a short man, he received more deliveries that could be pulled than other, taller batsmen, but nevertheless he rarely seemed to waste an opportunity. Australian batsmen by nature are good at the pull; it may be that the general standard of bowling is not quite so tight as it is in English county cricket. The average English seamer is so accurate that you can almost count the number of deliveries short enough to be pulled that you receive in an English season.

The force and power that are required to dispatch the short ball to the legside boundary must be tempered with timing and judgement when you are looking to score from similar deliveries on the offside. The late cut with which you send the ball down past the slips with a horizontal bat is a particularly delicate shot.

It is played to a short ball outside the off stump, which is steered down towards third-man. As with all shots played in this region, technique is of paramount importance because of the threatening presence of the 'keeper and the slips. As in all the other back-foot strokes, the first movement must be back and across; this time, however, the across movement is critical because you are aiming to reach a wide ball. If you do not move far enough towards the line, your eyes will be nowhere near a position from which they can accurately judge the pace and movement of the ball.

So the back foot must move wide to bring your head as near as possible to the line; you are leaning in to the shot rather than pulling away from it. With a full swing of a horizontal bat the ball is guided down to third man. If you have mastered the rolling of the wrists that we talked about in relation to the hook and the pull, you will have no problems about doing the same in the late cut. With the slips waiting like vultures to devour any chance, you must always cut over the ball.

The late cut is a positive shot, not just a little dab. By using the wrists you are adding force to the stroke, although it is not the brute force of the pull. Always cut hard at the ball; don't, as cricketers say, 'hang your bat out to dry', which means don't let it dangle limply outside the off stump. If you cut hard and mistime the shot, the pace you have put into the ball may carry it over the slips or make any catch

Peter Sainsbury, the Hampshire all-rounder, 'works' the ball on the leg-side . . . a popular way of gathering runs for professional batsmen, but one less recommended for the young cricketer (see Chapter 3)

The sweep, the ideal way to attack an off spinner on a turning wicket (see Chapter 3)

The pull ... the only shot in which the weight starts on the back foot and swings through on to the front foot as the stroke is completed (see Chapter 4)

The square cut, the perfect answer to a short ball outside the off stump. The wrists must be rolled to direct the ball downwards (see Chapter 4)

The cut is not exclusively a back-foot shot. You can improvise off the front foot to dispatch a loose delivery outside the off stump (see Chapter 4)

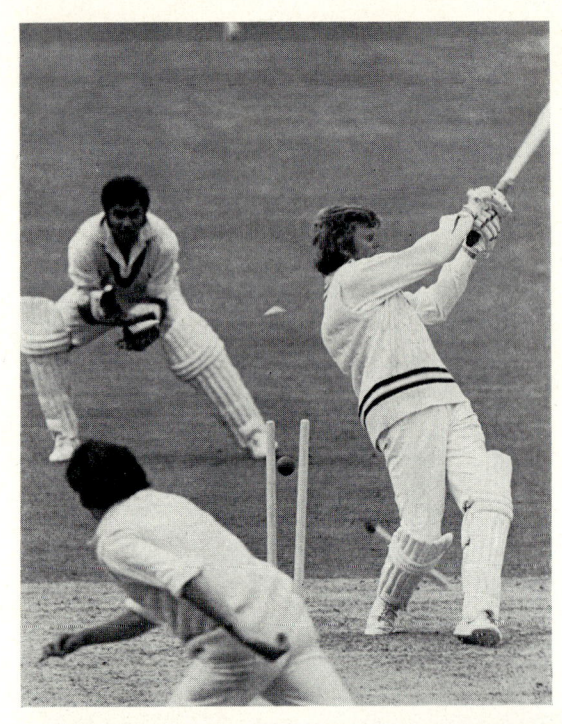

With a hundred on the board and a few overs left of a Gillette Cup tie, perhaps the only time that the old-fashioned heave can be truly justified. The result . . . a predictable one! Hampshire *v.* Lancashire, 1972

The author found leg-side shots difficult to master when he first played county cricket, and it took practice and application before he could confidently play shots like this one (see Chapter 5)

Attack off the Back Foot

too hot too hold. A snick off a limp bat will simply dolly into a close fielder's hands.

The square cut is the most positive version of the shot. Here you are really flashing the blade at the ball, trying to hit it, as the name of the shot implies, square with the wicket on the off-side. Really throw your arms into the shot, but in doing this don't lose sight of the cardinal principle of leaning your weight into it. Remember you are trying to hit the ball square; a common fault among young batsmen is to try to put so much force into the shot that they only succeed in crashing it straight into the ground. From there it trickles to cover or gully, there is no chance of a run and a lot of effort and a potentially scorable ball have been wasted. Obviously it is preferable to hit the ball into the ground rather than to slice it in the air for cover to catch, but if you think where you are trying to play the shot rather than just imparting power you are on the right lines.

I am not a great advocate of using a cut early in an innings, unless you receive a particularly bad ball. The chances of getting a snick are always there when you cut, but especially when you are not properly attuned to the pace of the bowling and the pitch. But when you are set, the cut is very effective against bowlers who are moving the ball away from the bat, like slow-left-arm spinners. The golden rule is never to play the cut to the men who bring the ball into the bat, because you are playing against the turn. There is one exception to this, I think; if you are set and an off-spinner tosses one up very wide of the stumps and you have been in for some time, then play the cut. Otherwise play straight.

Once again the way to perfect the whole range of attacking back-foot shots is to practise them. If you are finding any of them very difficult to perform, off you go to the nets and find yourself a patient pal who will bowl or throw the right type of delivery for you to practise the shot. If you are still struggling to master an attacking stroke after a lot of intensive work, and a coach has not been able to sort out your problems, cut the shot out.

But try to develop a working knowledge of every shot.

Think of your shots like the number of clubs in a golfer's bag; when he goes out to play a round he knows that he probably won't use them all, but he is well-equipped to cope with any situation he might encounter over the eighteen holes. You have to possess in your bag of shots something that will counter every type of delivery you are bowled, whether you have to attack or defend. Some you might have to use three balls an over, like the forward defensive, others only three times an innings, like the hook. But keep them in practice; the golfer, after all, is in terrible trouble if he produces a rusty club from his bag, but at worst he might drop a couple of shots. If your hook shot is rusty, it could well mean the end of an innings.

CHAPTER FIVE

Building an Innings

I am often asked by followers of first-class cricket why certain players rarely make big scores. Often these are batsmen who appear to have sound techniques and who always look impressive during their stay at the crease. Yet frequently this type of player is out for an elegantly made twenty-three when he has given every indication of going on to make a three-figure score. Why, the fans ask, does this always happen?

The very fact that such a question is asked highlights one area of learning to bat that every young cricketer must appreciate. A sound technique is undoubtedly the basis of batsmanship, but there is more to batting than just an instinctive ability to play shots. This serves you well enough in the nets, but it is an altogether different proposition out there in the middle. Look around your own school or club side and I almost guarantee that you can find a player who looks a world-beater in the nets but who rarely reproduces world-beating scores in matches.

Batting at the crease under competitive conditions requires application, concentration and general alertness. And it is these qualities – that can be summed up in the word 'temperament' – which are usually lacking in these players, whether at county or at club level. They flatter to deceive. It is the batsman who can combine the two 'Ts', Technique and Temperament, who will make the scores. After all, what is the game all about; it is the number of runs that are scored that matter, not how stylish you look at the wicket.

When you go out to bat you must be thinking positively. You must believe in yourself and resolve that you are going to do well. Obviously you are not going to score fifty every innings, but if you go out with the utmost determination you are going to make it that much harder for the bowler to get you back in the pavilion. Bowlers exist to a large extent on batsmen who simply give away their wickets. One lapse of concentration is often one too many and you are halfway towards the pavilion before you realise just what has happened. This is why in this respect cricket can be such a cruel game. You can be playing really well and perhaps you start to relax slightly too soon and you're out. It is this type of error that accounts for so many wickets that fall. It really has nothing to do with whether your forward defensive stroke is suspect or whether you played the sweep to the wrong ball; it is simply a matter of faulty concentration.

As far as temperament is concerned it is a very healthy sign to be nervous before you go out to bat. In first-class cricket there is not one person that I know who does not get nervous before he goes to the wicket, although some are much more tensed than others. I always feel the butterflies racing around my tummy as I put on the pads and they stay there usually until I have hit one or two deliveries in the middle of the bat and, of course, until I have got off the mark. From that point on one usually becomes attuned to the surroundings and begins to settle in. The danger, here, and I must stress this again, is not to become too confident too soon. You may be lucky enough to pick up a couple of boundaries early on, but don't allow them to go to your head. Remember, one mistake and you're back watching everybody else bat.

Begin your innings carefully, particularly if you are an opening batsman who has to face the new ball which is always likely to move about a little. But at the same time don't become so tied up with your nerves that you miss the opportunity to score from a particularly bad delivery. I certainly don't mean that you should launch yourself into a flowing off-drive to an outswinging delivery that looks as though it might be a half volley. That would be asking for trouble. But if, for instance, you are presented with a full toss second or third ball, hit it for four. It will make you feel much more comfortable and, of course, it will unsettle the bowler. So often, even at the higher levels of the game, you will see an opening batsman so obsessed with caution that he will allow long hops to pass through to the wicket-keeper and pat full tosses back to the bowler. I have no time for this approach. A bad ball is a bad ball at any time in your innings and it should get what it deserves.

But if you are not lucky enough to receive a poor delivery early on in your innings, look to start your score moving with quick running between the wickets. If there is an attacking field set for the bowler, with slips, gullies and short legs, there is often space in front of the wicket into which you can direct a defensive shot so that you quickly have one or two singles to your name. Try to begin each innings you play with this balance between defence and attack. Never lose your concentration, but never become so obsessed with pure survival that you cannot score a run. This is unfair to yourself, to your team and particularly to the batsman at the other end who has to think about scoring your share as well as his.

In limited-over cricket which is proving so popular now, playing yourself in assumes a different significance. In England there are the three sponsored competitions, the Gillette Cup limited to 60 overs a side, the Benson and Hedges Trophy at 55 overs, and regular Sunday John Player League at 40 overs each. Because of the popularity of this type of contest which always produces a win for one side or the other, school and club sides are beginning to play matches under these conditions. This does make for problems when you are batting because there is always the pressure of the number of overs slipping away. But I think that it has been proved that a slow, sound start is the basis on which a side can build a reasonable total.

If the openers take the first ten overs to move to around twenty, they are usually well set to accelerate and will probably treble the score in the next ten overs. So even in this type of cricket it does pay to play yourself in before committing yourself entirely to the attack. Obviously if you bat lower down the order, you have far less time to prepare for your onslaught against the bowling, but even then your chances of succeeding with a bout of slogging are much greater if you allow yourself a 'sighter' or two.

But whether you are playing to a number of overs or to the normal rules of the game, your own scoring rate and that of your side can be bolstered or spoiled depending on how well or how badly you run between the wickets. This is such an important part of run-getting and one that can be so easily overlooked; if you strike up an understanding with the players you bat with each week, you really can keep the score ticking along.

The essential factor in good running is clear, confident calling. If you say 'Yes' straightaway and you both sprint on the call, the chances of being run out are very small. The trouble comes with indecisive calling; once 'Yes, no, wait' is the theme of the conversation, one of you is likely to be continuing his run back to the pavilion. Only if there is a brilliant piece of fielding, followed by a direct throw to the stumps are you going to be run out if you both go on the call.

So if it is your call, shout loud and be positive. I am not a great believer in embroidering what you say with remarks like 'Come one' or 'Yes, there's two in this'. To me the call is either 'Yes', 'No', or 'Wait'. You might mention, as you pass your partner, something like, 'No arm' – meaning that the fielder chasing the ball cannot throw – or you might warn him as you cross that the fielder is left-handed. In this respect you must be alert and observant; study the fielders closely so that you know their strong and weak points. It is absolutely criminal if you play the ball to cover's left hand, go for a single and then find yourself run out by a left-handed throw. Even if you have never played against the chap before, you can soon pick his throwing arm by watching him in the field, or even noting with which hand he tosses the ball back to the bowler during an over.

Of course, there are rules laid down for calling and which batsman has the responsibility in each situation. If the ball goes behind the wicket it is the non-striker who calls, because he is in by far the best position to see what is happening. Conversely if the ball is struck in front of the wicket, the striker must take charge. Always stick to these guidelines, unless one batsman has a runner; in these circumstances it may be better for the other player to decide whether to run on every occasion.

Always sprint the first run; then if the fielder fumbles his pick-up or throws in wildly you are well positioned to capitalise on the error by grabbing another run. When there is obviously more than one run in the shot, try to turn so that you are facing the ball. If you are facing and you hit the ball through the covers, turn at the end of the first run towards the off-side so that you are grounding your bat behind the batting crease with your left hand. If there is three in it, turn for the third holding the bat now in the right-hand so that you can still easily focus on what is happening in the outfield. If you turn your back, there is just the possibility that you might be run out because you are not concentrating on what the fielder is doing.

Grounding your bat properly is also a must. Make sure it is behind the line, otherwise the umpire will signal one short and another opportunity will have been wasted. If you don't think this is important just imagine how you would feel if you were out for 99 and at sometime during your knock you had run one short. Always stretch to ground your bat so that you are cutting down the actual distance you have to run; you can probably reach a couple of yards, which will save you precious seconds. If you are sprinting to avoid being run out, slide your bat past the batting crease at full stretch in front of you. The bat must be on the ground otherwise you will be given out even if it is behind the crease in the air.

As far as running is concerned, you cannot relax once you are at the non-striker's end. As the bowler comes in, you must back-up, moving a yard or two down the pitch, so that if there is a quick run, you only have to race 20 yards instead of 22. That can make the difference between getting home or being stranded a couple of feet short.

When you have built up an instinctive understanding with

a team-mate, you will be able to take runs without even a call. The ball might hit your pads or drop down in front of you from a dead bat, and you are off. You know that he'll run and he knows that you will be coming, and you're home before any fielder can get a hand to the ball. This sort of running is very disruptive to the fielding side; the captain or the bowler might now want a man in short to stop these quick singles. This creates a gap somewhere else for you to look for your runs and the opposition have to make more decisions. You are now dictating to the fielding side.

The two best runners I have seen are Lee Irvine of Transvaal and Clive Radley of Middlesex; in fact Radley's nickname in England is 'The Run Thief' because of the way in which he steals runs that look absolutely impossible. He is very quick and goes for runs that I think 95 per cent of other county players would not even consider. I am sure that he obtains a far greater share of his runs in ones and twos than any other batsman; yet he is rarely run out because he has built up a shrewd understanding with the other members of the Middlesex side.

These are the type of players to learn from. If you have someone who is tremendously fast in your side, you will soon appreciate how easy it is to sneak these runs by batting regularly with him. In fact it can be quite frightening because it makes you realise just how many singles and twos you have missed in previous innings. If you have about 40 innings a season on average, as a county cricketer has, the number becomes quite staggering and these are runs that could have made the difference between losing and winning matches. Like good fielding, imaginative running between the wickets makes all the difference between good sides and bad sides. If you can snatch a run off four balls every over, you are moving along at a very healthy scoring rate, and you only need a few boundaries on top of that to be really cracking along.

Being adept at taking singles is one way to free yourself from another batting problem, that of going through a run of low scores. However successful you are it happens sooner or later and it is a great test of your temperament and perseverance. I remember the great Peter May having a terrible time when he led the M.C.C. team to South Africa in 1956-57 and although we were all very pleased that our players were getting him out regularly I remember feeling very disappointed that we didn't see the best of him in the Test Matches.

I had a bad time during the 1971 season. I got nought in the second innings against Sussex and then we played Essex in the next match on a very difficult pitch and I landed a 'pair'. The next match was at Lords against Middlesex and I really had to feel my way back into form. By taking things very carefully I managed to make fifty odd in the first innings and eighty in the second.

The most important thing is not to allow yourself to become depressed and pessimistic. However well you are playing a brilliant catch or a beautiful delivery can have you back in the pavilion, and if this happens three or four innings running you just have to become more and more determined that you will break this 'bad trot'. Before you go into bat have a net or ask a team-mate to throw a ball at you – and do this for a longer time than you might normally do before an innings.

It is no good, either, just sitting back and saying to yourself that it will all come right. You must go out to the wicket really purposefully, saying to yourself that no matter what happens you are going to score runs. It might take you a little longer than normal, but even if you are batting badly stick it out until you finally find yourself middling the ball again. If you find yourself bogged down during this period of readjustment, don't throw your wicket away with a mighty slog that is designed to get the scoreboard moving again. As I have said, look to the quick single to increase your total. Not only is it far less likely to cost you your wicket, it will create the gaps in the field for you to exploit with boundaries.

One final word of advice. Always learn from your experience as a batsman. Every time you go to the wicket you are increasing your knowledge of what we have seen to be a complex art. Particularly pay attention to the ways in which you are dismissed and try to eliminate the faults in your game that have cost you your wicket. In an earlier chapter I have told you how Mike Procter solved his problems outside the off stump and if you analyse your own play you can improve immensely by practising hard. If you are always out bowled, there is something suspect about your defensive technique; perhaps that deadly gap appears between pad and bat or you may be tending to play across the line. If you are not sure ask your coach or even the chap who was at the other end when you were out, or the umpire who would have been in an excellent position to see. If you do not attend to these details you are going to continue to make the same mistakes – with the same disturbing results.

When I first came to England to play county cricket, I wasn't a good leg-side player, but I found that on the slower pitches over here all the successful English players were strong off their legs. Also there were many more off-spin and inswing bowlers bringing the ball into my pads, so I just had to learn about leg-side technique and bring it into my game. Every time I went to the crease I was faced with this problem, and after every knock I would look back on how I had managed to cope with it. Eventually it became second nature, but the important point was to recognise this need and work at it.

As a batsman going in number three downwards, you can also learn from your colleagues' experience in each match. Whereas the openers may not know anything about the opening bowlers that they must face, at number three you can sit and watch while they find out and try to assess just what the bowler is trying to do. His field placing is one clue; if he has a lot of slips he is trying to move the ball away from the bat; if there are several close fielders on the leg side, then you can expect the ball to slant into you. Watch his run up; try to assess his pace; note whereabouts he delivers the ball from; does he appear to have a slower ball in his repertoire? All these little points will make it that much easier for you when it is your turn to go out to bat.

This, then, is the recipe for successful batting. Develop your technique and approach the task with a sound temperament and a willingness to do the very best you can. It won't always work – the skill of the bowlers, the fielders and luck will see to that – but with these principles you have every chance of becoming a regular run-getter. Without them you are sunk.

CHAPTER SIX

The Basics of Bowling

'Watch me, sir. I'm Mike Procter.' 'Look at this, coach. Aren't I like John Snow?' These are the type of remarks that I hear so often from young cricketers when I am holding a coaching session. And to me they so often hold the key to the development of the bowlers of the future.

Because the great bowlers of the day can be so easily copied with their distinctive run-ups, actions and follow throughs, schoolboys are always tempted to seek success by trying directly to mimic the methods of their heroes. What they must realise is that in doing so they are distorting much of their own natural bowling ability.

Of course, I am not for one moment suggesting that you cannot learn from the players you watch on the television or at the first-class cricket grounds. They can teach you much. What I am saying is that the art of bowling requires so much co-ordination of mind and muscle that it is much better for you to use and develop your own natural style than it is for you to try to become a mirror-image of whomever you admire most.

Having issued that word of warning, there are certain basic facets of bowling which, if you master them, will take you a long way towards becoming a consistent performer with the ball. Whether you aspire to be a ferocious fast bowler or a spinner of guile and patience, establish a rhythmic run-up that leads you into a balanced action and a correct follow-through and you have taken a big step towards becoming a scourge to the batsmen.

Returning to the problem of copying famous bowlers, it is perhaps in the run-up that youngsters are most guilty, especially when it comes to bowling quick. I remember only too well from my days at Durban High School the sort of butterflies I used to feel when I saw an opening bowler pace out a run of around 25 yards. But as I grew older I realised that more often than not these whirlwind merchants either rushed in so quickly that they had little control over what happened when they reached the crease or they became tired so soon from such a punishing run that they lost any pace they gained from such an approach.

When we talk about the bowling action, you will see that you can generate pace and power from the body, particularly the back and the shoulders. Therefore the run-up should be geared to building up a rhythm that leads you into the delivery stride in a forceful but controlled position. I really feel that for most young fast bowlers there is never any need to extend the approach to more than 15 or 16 yards.

There are those fast bowlers in county and Test cricket who do go way beyond this mark. Mike Procter is one, John Price of Middlesex and England is another; the Australian paceman Dennis Lillee also comes racing in to bowl from around the 30 yard mark. I have had long talks with 'Prockie' about this and he maintains that those extra yards help establish this all-important rhythm. Mike is undoubtedly a world-class bowler and he is the best judge of what suits him, but I have seen him bowl every bit as quick off a vastly reduced run.

If you want an example of exceptional pace generated off a relatively short, rhythmic approach to the bowling crease, then look no further than John Snow. Any Test batsman in the cricket-playing world will tell you that he really is quick, but anyone facing him for the first time could be forgiven for expecting a delivery of around medium pace as Snow jogs briskly in to bowl. Consequently he can bowl as many overs at top pace in a spell as any paceman I have ever seen, which has been a fantastic help to the England side.

So if you are a fast bowler, analyse this problem and try to work at the run-up that suits you best, bearing in mind that not only do you want to fire away with quick deliveries but that you want control, accuracy and to be able to sustain your assault on the opposition for longer than a couple of lightning overs. You may well find that you can embrace all these factors from a run of around 15 paces.

This is not a problem confined to the fast bowlers' union. Slow bowlers, too, must work out an approach that establishes a tempo for their task, but the problem here is not one of run-ups too long. Far from it. It is possible to deliver an accurate off-spinner or leg-break from a standing position or a one-pace run, but bowling is not just a case of letting the ball go. You should be aiming to gain momentum so that you arrive at the crease at the right time to deliver the ball. In this respect I think it is vital for a spin bowler to move in a few paces before bowling.

This rhythm is often reflected in the amount of pace or 'nip' off the wicket that the ball has after it has pitched. You'll find that a slow delivery tossed down from a standing position will more often than not just come gently through on to the bat, whereas a delivery of equal pace through the air bowled from a rhythmic run up will hurry on a little extra and that may be enough to beat the bat. Both Ray Illingworth and Derek Underwood, two of the most devastating spinners in county cricket, bowl off quite long runs and both of them have this quality in their bowling: that they can hurry the ball on to you. I don't think that young players need such a lengthy approach to the wicket, but there must be a defined run, not just a shuffle of a pace-and-a-half.

In running in to bowl you are facing chest-on or square-on to the wicket and to the batsman. But once you reach the wicket and commence your bowling action in the delivery stride, you are back to that old chestnut that cricket is a sideways game. From being front-on you must twist your body into a side-on delivery position. There will be slight variations in style, depending on what you are trying to bowl and at what pace, but this basic action depends on the batsman seeing your front shoulder at the point of delivery and not your chest.

To turn side-on as you approach the crease, place your back foot (the right if you are a right-handed bowler, the left if you are a left-armer) parallel to the crease so that the toes are pointing out on the leg-side rather than straight at the batsman. At that moment all your weight is on that foot, and already you are moving into the sideways position. Now take the final pace forward with your front foot, making sure not to overstep the crease, throwing it across in front of the back foot with the toes pointing towards leg slip. You should now have your front shoulder pointing straight at the batsman.

At the same time, whilst you are on the back foot, your front arm, the non-bowling arm, comes up, with the hand pointing vertically upwards, and straightens. As the weight transfers on to the front foot, this arm drops down whilst the bowling arm comes up to let the ball go at the top of the arc. All the while you must keep your head still with your eyes focused on the direction in which the ball is being propelled.

The position of the front arm in relation to your head is crucial. As it is lifted you should be looking at the batsman outside the arm, and not underneath; otherwise you cannot possibly be perfectly side-on. This movement also forces you to arch your back, which will help you to put your body strength behind every ball you bowl. Never think of bowling as just a skill of the arms and hands. You use your shoulders, your back and even the power in your thighs.

Try to keep the bowling arm as high as possible. The classic test, here, is to check how near it is to your ear as it comes over the top; ideally the area around the bicep muscles should just brush the side of your head. And when your arm is at its highest point, this is the time to let the ball go. If you let it go before then, your arm is still on the upswing and the ball will continue to go upwards, providing the batsman with the sort of full toss he dreams about. If you hold on to the ball too long, the arm is now coming down its swing and the ball must also go down. The result? A long hop that once more will have the batsman licking his lips.

One bowler whose action I thoroughly admire is the former England all-rounder, Tom Cartwright. His control over the ball at medium pace is exemplary, and I am convinced that this is because his is the sort of action that justifies all the advice that you can ever read in a text-book. His arm always comes over high, and I can hardly ever remember receiving a bad ball from him.

Not all bowlers are so orthodox – which brings me back again to Mike Procter. He is always pointed out as being the chap who bowls off the wrong foot, but this is only half true. His front foot is on its way down into a relatively orthodox position, but it is still in the air when he lets the ball go. It puts a lot of strain on his back, but he prefers it and his figures speak for themselves. The strangest part of it is that Mike is not a complete freak. He can also bowl in a most orthodox way, and occasionally, when he is called upon to bowl spinners for Gloucestershire or Rhodesia, you will see him turning his arm over in the more normal way.

In my experience as a coach, I have come across one or two boys who do bowl off the wrong foot quite naturally. Here the player and the coach are faced with an awkward decision; the unorthodox style is physically demanding and may eventually cause injuries; yet in trying to switch to a more natural method the player may lose the gifts and talents he is displaying in the other vein. There really can be no hard and fast rules about what to do, but I think any bowler with an eccentric streak to his style must think hard about changing before he finally opts to continue as before.

One quality that Mike Procter's technique does not prevent him from exhibiting is a strong follow-through, and this is another essential to all types of bowlers. As you release the ball, the back leg comes through to the front once more and you take a couple more firm paces before coming to a halt. As the bowling arm comes down after releasing the ball, carry its swing through to the furthest point bringing it right across your body until the hand is directed to the turf.

In following-through, of course, make sure that you veer away from the batting strip, otherwise you will be warned by the umpire for scarring the surface and, if you persist, your captain will be ordered to take you off.

Although it may cause one or two problems at home, you can check your action for all these various points in front of the full-length mirror, which should by now be an old friend. If there is room, run up a couple of paces, let loose an imaginary ball and then allow yourself another few feet to follow-through. Begin in slow motion, going through each stage slowly. Then gradually increase the speed until you are doing everything at the pace you would perform at in a match. If you find difficulty in focusing at the mirror, then there are definitely faults in your action; almost certainly you are not keeping that head still.

Being satisfied with your action is only the starting point of bowling. From there you have to learn to control the ball, to be able to land it at will wherever you are aiming to pitch each delivery. No one can achieve total precision but you are looking to be sufficiently competent to be, as we say in the first-class dressing-rooms, 'there or thereabouts'.

To achieve this amount of accuracy there is no short cut. You have to practise. And you must practise regularly. Go out to the nets on your own with a ball and bowl at one stump. Before you start, make a mark on a good length – and by this I mean that area on which any delivery pitched there will force the batsman to play a defensive shot. You can either put down a sheet of paper about nine inches square or even a handkerchief; this is your target to hit. Place it on a length in front of the stump, so that if you hit the spot the chances are you will hit the wicket.

If you are lucky enough to have a net especially for bowlers, you can heavily water a patch of similar size to the handkerchief. When the ball pitches on this spot it will take away a little of the top surface and leave marks that will testify to your accuracy.

This spot, then, becomes your target over and over again. First of all you must cultivate the ability to hit it at will with your stock delivery, the ball you regularly bowl best.

C

Then sharpen your marksmanship with all your varieties. Bowl over and around the wicket, varying that with the ball delivered wide of the crease and the one that you run close to the stumps to bowl. Keep hammering away at that spot with your quicker delivery, so that you don't fall into the easy trap of dropping short every time you strive for more pace. Try to be absolutely spot-on with the slower ball, the one you hold back a little. In fact any type of ball, you wish to bowl in a match, with the exception of the bumper and the yorker which require separate practice, learn to land it on this good length.

One way to make the practice that much more interesting is to work with six or eight balls, depending on whether you play to the six or eight ball over rules. Bowl out an over, striving to land on that spot with each delivery. Then walk up the wicket to collect the balls; this will give a little rest and time to analyse how well you are doing. Collect the balls and then bowl another over, and another, and another. Six out of six is the standard you are aiming for, and you shouldn't be satisfied until you achieve that consistently.

Take a look at all the successful Test Match bowlers and this is perhaps their most important quality. Illingworth and Underwood, I have already mentioned; their control is magnificent. Underwood because he is that little bit quicker through the air is almost impossible to come down the wicket to play because his length is unwavering. The actual mechanics of his bowling are as good as any I have ever seen; he is an absolute craftsman. Of the quicker men John Snow is very accurate and Geoff Arnold I have a great respect for; he always seems to be in command of where the ball is going to pitch. In South Africa Peter Pollock, a world class fast bowler for ten years, was incredibly accurate for one so quick, and I am a big fan of Vincent van der Bijl, who is well over six feet, and hammers the ball down on a length. I think he would really set English county cricket alight if he decides to come over.

With this mastery of control you will then be able to pitch the ball around any spot you are aiming for. You will soon discover that what is, in theory, a good length in the nets might not be out in the middle. Length and direction do become directly related to two factors, the nature of the batsman who is facing and the type of ball you want to send down. For example if you are bowling to a tall fellow, he might be able to turn your good length net delivery into a half volley, so a good length to him is a little shorter. Similarly you might have been pitching middle stump in practice, but if you are bowling an off-break or an inswinger you will be looking to direct your attack further towards the off stump.

We will cover these more specific instances in the following chapters, but there are two final general tips that will help you in school cricket. It is always better to keep the ball up to the bat rather than to pitch it short; young players are by and large much more natural pullers than drivers, so they are less likely to punish a half volley than a long hop. Secondly, it will usually be more profitable to bowl at the off stump than on the leg side for more or less the same reason. The natural stroke to the young cricketer is not the off-drive, it is the swing to leg.

As with batting; the basics of bowling must never be neglected. Every building must have a solid foundation, and the art of bowling takes a lot of construction. With a command of length and direction allied to a comfortable run up and a controlled action, you are on your way. Now is the time to make the ball work for you. . . .

CHAPTER SEVEN

Fast and Medium Pace Bowling

There is undoubtedly something glamorous about being a genuinely fast bowler. The crowds love to see the smooth, rhythmic approach of the real quickie, and a hush always descends over the ground as he pounds in to bowl. Like a centre-forward in soccer, every youngster longs at some time to be a real paceman, dreaming of making batsmen shake in their boots as he runs in to bowl.

Unfortunately it is not as simple as that. The higher the grade of cricket you play, the less you will find sheer pace to be effective. Whereas you might, if you are lucky, terrify one or two sides out in school cricket, you will have to be startlingly quick if you wish to make the same impression when you begin to compete at more senior levels. In first-class cricket there are very few players who are really quick. John Snow and Mike Procter are on the sharp side; Yorkshire's Chris Old is another who can make you hurry a little. Warwickshire's Bob Willis, at six foot and a half, is another with the physique that could turn him into a real paceman.

But these bowlers do not succeed simply because they hurl the ball down at around 80 miles per hour; most players with a sound technique are quite equal to that. They use the ball. They make it swing in the air. On pitching they make it dart about off the seam. They have control of line and length. And they vary their pace.

If you want to become a pace bowler, this is the first thing you must realise. It is more than a case of just rushing up to the wicket and letting the ball go. You have to learn to make the ball work for you. And the slower your pace the more you must rely on any movement you can obtain in the air and off the pitch.

The next time you have the opportunity, take a good look at a new ball. Get the feel of it, and take notice of the facets that are going to help you. The shiny red surface will help you swing the ball through the air; the thick weaving of the seam will give you the movement off the pitch. As the ball becomes older throughout a match, these are the attributes that you must try to maintain. Always try to keep one side of the ball shiny by polishing it on your flannels; it is against the rules to pick and probe at the seam, but you can do your best to ensure that it does not become flattened by not allowing the batsmen to play aggressive shots to your bowling.

The aerodynamics of swing bowling mystify most experts, but the most accepted and acceptable theory is that the shiny ball moves through the air quicker than an old ball. Thus if one half of the ball is shiny and one is dull, the shiny side will pull the ball to one side and cause swing. On top of this, most county bowlers, who are by and large a superstitious bunch, believe that the shiny side should be the one with less imprinted letters, like the maker's name and the size and weight, on it. The letters are supposed to interfere with swing. As an off-spinner, who does not get as much bowling as he would like, I am in no position to disagree with the wisdom of the professional bowler.

Therefore if you are a right-arm bowler, the following principles apply. If you hold the ball with the seam vertical with the shiny side on the right the ball will swing from right to left, or from leg to off to a right-handed batsman; this is the outswinger. Conversely if the shiny side is on the left, the ball will swing from right to left and become an inswinger to a right-hander.

To convert the principles into practice, you must pay account to slight changes in how you grip the ball and to your body action. Swing bowling can be an elusive art. Sometimes the ball will wobble about all over the place; on other occasions it will hardly deviate at all. Often the weather is an important factor – on a humid morning at Bournemouth it is sometimes like batting against a boomerang – but sometimes the bowler loses that little snap in his action that gives each delivery the swerve.

The outswinger is undoubtedly the more dangerous delivery. The ball leaving the bat can so often induce an error in judging the line of trajectory. The result is an outside edge and a probable chance to the slips or the wicket-keeper. If you can learn to make the ball curve away towards the slip, you are going to be a dangerous paceman, especially with the new ball.

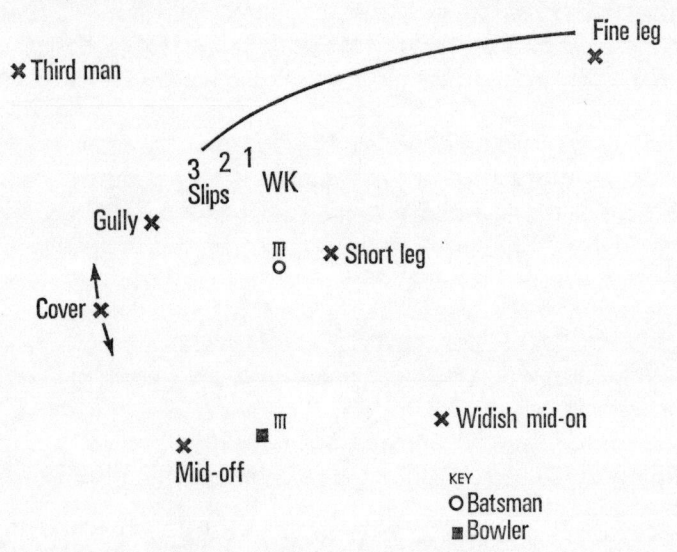

Fig. 1. Field for outswing bowlers. If the ball is not swinging a lot 3rd slip can drop to fine leg

Pick up the ball, keeping, as I have said, the shinier side on the right with the seam pointing vertically or perhaps slightly, but only slightly, pointing towards the slips. The grip involves only the first two fingers and the thumb. Place the two fingers vertically down the seam so that its centre is between the two of them, whilst the thumb comes underneath the ball again holding the seam. Don't grip too tightly or you will find that it will stick to your fingers when you come to releasing it.

What you are aiming to do is to propel the ball down the wicket in such a way that the seam remains vertical all the time. So you can see that if you do not release it cleanly it will pull to one side and any chance of it swinging will virtually disappear. The best way to ensure that this does not happen is to cock your wrist back as your arm reaches its highest point; then as you actually let the ball go, run your fingers down it keeping that seam upright.

The quality of your action will also help the outswing. Try to get completely side-on; really throw that front foot across your body in the last stride so that your front shoulder is leading you into each delivery. Finally, allow yourself a complete follow-through.

Because I am an opening batsman and continually exposed to the problems of dealing with the swinging ball, I am well qualified to testify to the effectiveness of the outswinger. Any player, no matter what his standard, is a little vulnerable to this type of ball early in his innings and bowlers like Geoff Arnold and the Australian sensation of 1972, Bob Massie, pick up a large proportion of their wickets caught behind the wicket or in the slips.

With all swing bowling, it is essential to keep the ball up to the bat to give it the maximum opportunity to swing through the air and to draw the batsman forward into a false stroke. If you drop short he will be able to play back and watch the movement right on to the bat. The best line, which may vary depending on the individual player you are bowling at, is around middle and middle and off. If you aim the delivery there, the batsman will be forced to play a shot and you are hoping that the swing will drift it away from the bat and flick the edge before going through. If you bowl at the off stump or just outside, the swing will carry the ball past the off stump and the batsman can safely pad up and let it pass. Conversely if you aim too wide at around leg stump, the swing, because of the angle of flight, can at best only straighten the ball up, and you have much less chance of forcing the ball past a forward defensive shot.

The major exception to this comes if you are looking to slip in a yorker, the ball aimed to pitch right in the blockhole. This is the one to fire in at the leg stump. I think I speak for all openers when I tell you that this is the hardest delivery in the world to play. It really is very difficult, particularly if you are tall, to slam your bat down on such a ball. The swing will ensure that the yorker doesn't slide away down the leg-side, but crashes into the middle and leg stumps. For the outswing bowler it is almost as much the perfect dismissal as the little nicked catch to wicket-keeper.

If you have the opportunity to watch someone like Geoff Arnold in action, you will soon notice that once you have mastered the pure outswinger you can vary your line from time to time. For example, he might bowl one or two widish outswingers that the batsman can watch complacently as they pass harmlessly to the keeper, then he might bowl another of similar line that whips back in off the pitch. The unwary batsman is expecting it to pass by and might well lose his off stump or depart to an l.b.w. decision.

The inswinger is perhaps slightly easier to bowl and also likely to bring you wickets, particularly under the present l.b.w. ruling. The danger is that the ball will swing too much to hit the stumps and that the batsman will be given a free swing at anything that passes down the leg side.

The grip is similar to that of the outswinger, but this time open the two fingers slightly more and angle the seam a little towards leg slip. The first finger is now completely on the left-hand-side of the ball, the shiny half, whereas the middle finger runs along and slightly across the seam. Again cock the wrist, this time back and in towards you so that you are almost pushing the ball in at a right-handed batsman.

You can open up your body action a little; don't become chest-on but you can pull the front shoulder a few inches towards the off-side. As long as your arm is kept high, this will aid the inswing. To avoid this problem of the inswinger passing uselessly down the leg-side, aim it outside the off stump so that each delivery is designed to hit the stumps. Under the l.b.w. rule, batsmen can be out if the ball pitches

Fast and Medium Pace Bowling 73

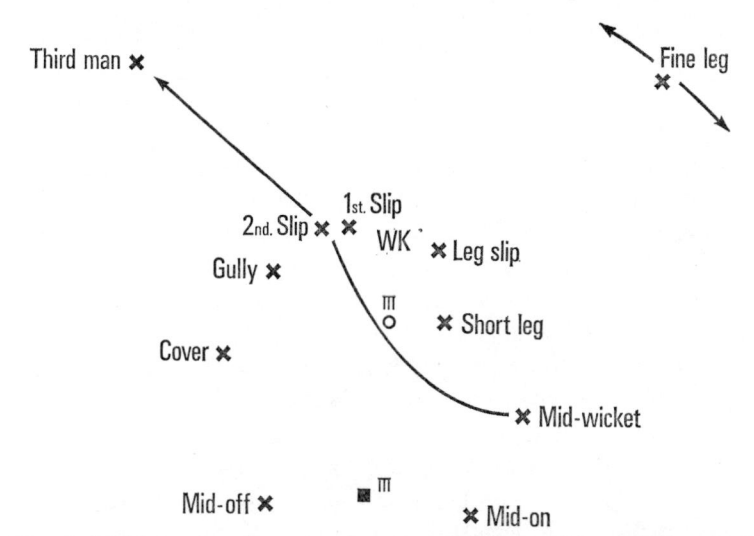

```
Third man ✖                                    ↖ Fine leg
         ↖                                       ✖
                                                   ↘

                    1st. Slip
          2nd. Slip ✖  ✖
                       WK    ✖ Leg slip
         Gully ✖
                        ▥
                        o    ✖ Short leg

          Cover ✖

                                    ✖ Mid-wicket

       Mid-off ✖      ▪ ▥
                                ✖ Mid-on
```

Fig. 2. Field for inswinger bowler. Depending on the conditions and the state of the game, the second slip can drop down to third man, or come across to mid-wicket

outside the off stump and hits the pads in line between the two sets of stumps, provided the ball is going to hit the wicket of course.

So often, if your line drifts towards middle stump, you are going to hit the pads without any chance of winning an l.b.w. decision. Quite rightly the umpire will give the batsman the benefit of the doubt because the odds are that the ball would have curved away past the leg stump. Many top-line inswing bowlers have a favourite trick that enables them to counteract this problem.

They run up and bowl what looks to be exactly the standard inswinging delivery – the same grip, the same run up, the same action, the same follow-through. But instead of holding the ball with the shiny side to the left, they switch it round to the right. This holds up the swing and should produce a completely straight delivery. After sending three or four overs of varying degrees of inswing, the batsman may well feel totally safe about aiming an attacking shot to any delivery starting around middle or middle and leg stumps. As soon as he shows signs of looking to force deliveries that pitch on the stumps away on the leg-side, he becomes a candidate for the straight one and there is a strong possibility that you might knock over his castle or send him back l.b.w.

When Bob Massie took sixteen wickets in the Lord's Test of the 1972 England versus Australia series, he gave an almost faultless display of swing bowling. He utterly confounded the England batting by moving the ball both ways in the air, and, from watching it on the television, I felt sure that very few of the home batsmen could 'read' the direction of the swing. But if you are a young swing bowler, perhaps the greatest lesson Massie's display held for you was the way he wobbled the ball so late in flight.

If the ball starts to swing from the moment it leaves your hand, then the batsman has the maximum time to assess the degree of the movement. The later it begins to curve, the less time he has to adjust.

Whilst the seam on a cricket ball will help you swing it through the air, it also enables you to get some lateral movement after you have pitched it into the wicket. In seaming or cutting the ball off the wicket, you are aiming to make the ball bounce on the seam so that it nips in from the off or angles away towards the slips.

Like the outswinger, the leg cutter can be devastating because the ball moves away from the bat. John Snow has cultivated the ability to bowl this type of delivery almost as his stock ball; he drifts the ball into a right-hander with a little inswing and then cuts it away off the seam. At his pace this is perhaps the hardest delivery to counter that any seam bowler can produce.

Again the grip and wrist action are of primary importance. Hold the ball seam upwards as you would do to swing it, but this time the middle finger is vital. Place it along the seam, angling it slightly across so that the top joint is slightly to the right; the first finger holds the left side of the ball, again running parallel to the seam, whilst the thumb grips underneath and the other two fingers are tucked down out of the way.

As you let the ball go, cock the wrist and then flick your fingers hard across the ball from right to left; as the first finger comes down, the ball is almost totally controlled by the middle finger. Almost invariably when you first try to bowl this ball in the nets, you will pitch short because in making this cutting movement the tendency is to drag the ball down into the pitch. But concentrate on letting the ball go at the top of your arm swing, and this will help you keep the ball pitched up. If you do drop short, the batsman will be able to get on to the back foot and counter that movement you have worked hard to achieve.

To move the ball the other way, into the bat, you must develop the off cutter, which looks like a fast off break, but the ball is cut rather than spun. Hold the ball up in front of you with the seam running from eight o'clock to two o'clock; then place your first two fingers vertically around the ball, so that they are running across the seam. The right side of the top joint of the middle finger is now pressed against the edge of the seam.

The cutting movement is the reverse of the leg cutter; you are flicking your fingers from left to right, pushing the middle finger hard against the seam. Again you must make sure that you do not dig the ball into the pitch nearer you than the batsman; always try to bring the batsman forward because you are committing him. If the ball does do a little off the seam, he is not in such a good position to adjust; once he is on the back foot he has the chance to gauge the movement off the pitch.

Whatever type of delivery is your stock ball, as a pace bowler you will want to be able to vary the speed at which you bowl, and a slower ball is a valuable weapon. It is not just enough, however, to run up and then bring your arm up slower and let the ball go. Any batsman worth his salt will pick this out easily. What's more he will probably hit it for four, because this sort of attempt will so disrupt your rhythm that you will end up delivering a slow full toss or long hop.

The secret, as with all methods of strategic bowling, is to make the batsman think that he is going to face your stock delivery once more. The method of slipping in a slower ball that I favour is to release the ball just before your arm reaches the top of its swing. Another method is to hold the ball in the palm of your hand rather than the fingers, and just run up and bowl as normal. But I am not a great advocate of this because an observant player will spot the change of grip and be ready to cope with the change of pace.

Not only must you try to deceive the batsman at the point of delivery, you must also land the ball on the same spot that you usually aim for. This is perhaps the crux of the problem, the ability to control the slower ball. It is only something that can come with practice, and therefore I would most strongly advise you against bowling this type of delivery spontaneously during a game if you haven't put in the work in the nets. But, bowled properly, it can easily make the batsman play too soon and perhaps spoon up a catch.

Bowling a slower ball has rarely got any bowler into trouble, but hurling down bumpers is a much more controversial subject. Many famous fast bowling names from Harold Larwood to Wes Hall, and even recently Mike Procter, have incurred the wrath of opponents and sometimes the umpires, for using the ball that pitches short and flies up at the batsman's head. Nevertheless, as someone who has faced his fair share of bouncers from most of the world's big guns, I would say that the bumper is essential to the repertoire of any quick bowler.

By this I do not mean there should be persistent physical intimidation of the batsman. That is not only against the laws, it is also thoroughly bad sportsmanship, and anyone who consistently infringes the rules will soon run out of clubs willing to give him a game. But having made that reservation, I am sure that, sparingly used, the bouncer is a perfectly fair delivery and that once in a while it is perfectly legitimate to try to unsettle an opponent in this way.

But as with any delivery, it must be well thought out and well controlled. Any good player will have no problem avoiding a bouncer if it is either too high or too wide. And since you are mustering all your physical resources to try to get the ball to lift, it is downright stupid to waste all that energy. The ideal bouncer should get up about head high, or no more than six inches above this, and should be directed around middle and leg stump; this will compel a reaction from the batsman. He has to duck or sway out of the way, or try to make contact with his bat. And if he does get his bat to the ball, the height of the bounce will make it very difficult for him to direct the ball into the ground.

As you might expect, the fast bowlers who have caused me the most problems with bouncers are those who generally have shown marvellous control for quick bowlers. Peter Pollock bowled a splendid bouncer – and I don't just say that because he landed me one above the eye; I remember in 1965 Peter caught John Edrich a nasty blow on the forehead with a lifting delivery at Lord's. No bowler likes to inflict pain on opponents but I think even John would admit that it was skilful bowling on Peter's part. John Snow and Mike Procter are also masters of the bumper; both use them discreetly because, as with any variation, it ceases to become a variation if it is used too often.

The bouncer has a dual effect. It might gain you a wicket directly, but you may unsettle your opponent to such an extent that you capture his scalp soon after. The most respected combination of deliveries that the great Fred Trueman used to such good purpose was to slip in the well-directed bouncer and follow it with a fast yorker pitched right in around middle and leg stumps.

This worked for Fred many times and it will work for you if you can master the control that is so vital. A bouncer badly bowled can become a gift of a long hop; a poorly directed yorker will end up as an inviting full toss. The moral should be clear enough by now. Whatever type of pace bowler you want to be, and obviously one of the techniques we have discussed will be your particular favourite, you must practise until you can produce your basic delivery at will. From there begin to develop your variations, the slower ball, the yorker, the bumper, the one bowled from 23 yards and so on; if you are trying to swing the ball, learn to master the off cutter so that you have the means to deceive your opponents. Bowlers have to be a patient breed not only in the middle but in the amount of hours given up to nets as well.

CHAPTER EIGHT

Spin Bowling

When I was over in England with the South African Schools' side in 1963, perhaps our toughest match was at The Oval against a side glittering with Test players. There I had my first encounter with the Australian Test captain Richie Benaud, who at that time was the best leg-spinner in the world.

I must admit I was a little apprehensive as Richie came on to bowl at me, but when he dropped one short I pulled it through mid-wicket for four; what a piece of cake, I thought to myself. The next ball was exactly the same, short once more, and again I whacked it to the fence. He ran into bowl again and pitched on exactly the same spot; instinctively I moved into position for the pull. But before my bat had started its downswing, the ball had clipped the top of the middle stump. Without any apparent change of action, he had bowled a much quicker delivery, his top-spinner or 'flipper', that had simply fizzed off the pitch and beaten me completely.

Although for a young batsman this was an impressive lesson in how to cope, or rather how not to cope, with spin bowling, it was a supreme example to an aspiring spinner, as I was, of the science of the skill. On this occasion my wicket had cost Benaud eight runs; to snare a more experienced player it would have cost more. But with controlled spin, allied to variations in length and flight plus plenty of cunning and guile, Benaud would hunt down his prey.

As a spinner, bowling at a slower pace, you are more

Spin Bowling

vulnerable than the quicker bowlers to punishment if you stray in line or length. In addition, if you are really trying to give the ball a spin, rather than just letting it roll out of your hand, you will find it hard to maintain control, at first. So the message for the young spin bowler is crystal clear – practise, practise, practise. Whether you specialise in off breaks, leg-spin, slow left-arm, googlies or chinamen, learn to pitch on that good length. On such a solid foundation you will be well equipped to widen your range to include the subtle skills of the kind Richie Benaud used to deceive me.

The off spinner and the orthodox slow left-arm bowlers are the most common types of slow bowlers, because the delivery spun from the fingers is much easier to control than the wrist and finger combination used by leg spinners. The off break turns the ball in towards the right-handed batsman, whilst the slow left-arm is really bowling the same delivery in reverse, turning it away from the bat.

With swing and seam bowling the ball is basically gripped with the seam upright, but for spinning the seam will now run horizontally across the first two fingers. And whereas the pace bowler must hold it relatively loosely, the spinner must wrap his fingers round the ball, not so tightly that it cannot be released easily, but nevertheless firmly enough to impart the spin.

In the off break, the first finger does the work. You have often heard or read that 'so-and-so', the county off spinner, is

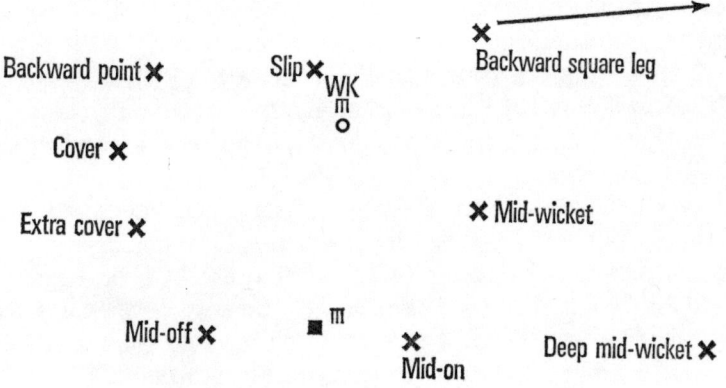

Backward point ✗ Slip ✗ Backward square leg
                    WK
                    m
                    o
Cover ✗

Extra cover ✗   ✗ Mid-wicket

        Mid-off ✗   ▪ m
                        ✗   Deep mid-wicket ✗
                      Mid-on

Fig. 3. Field for off spin on a good wicket

Fig. 4. Field for off spin on a turning wicket

unable to play because of a sore spinning finger. This is because the inside of the top joint of the first finger has rubbed raw from continually pushing hard against the seam to gain the maximum amount of turn. Hold the ball in the first two fingers, spreading them as wide as you can without losing control of what you are trying to do. The other two fingers are tucked into the palm, well out of the way, whilst the thumb is also held back away from the ball.

As you bring your arm up to its highest point in the delivery stride, cock the wrist back, and then as you let go of the ball push hard with the first finger to the right and the second fingers snaps down the right hand side of the ball into your palm. As the ball leaves your hand it should be spinning quickly in a clockwise direction. On pitching this movement will carry the ball from your left to your right, in other words into the batsman.

Try to keep completely sideways-on as you deliver the ball. It will not only help you bowl straight, but because your arm comes over in the correct position you will be able to give the ball a real tweak.

The ideal line for an off spinner depends on how much the ball is turning. On a good wicket you should be aiming to pitch on or just outside the off stump, so that the ball, on turning, will hit the sticks. Like the inswing bowler, once you start pitching on middle and leg stumps you have no chance of hitting the wicket, unless of course you are bowling a ball that goes straight through. But if the ball is turning and you have to

Text-book action from Australian fast bowler Dennis Lillee. Notice how he looks at the batsman from behind his front arm, thus ensuring the beautifully balanced side-on delivery (see Chapter 6)

Not one to copy! Yet Mike Procter has achieved success at the highest levels using his eccentric technique of bowling off the 'wrong' foot (see Chapter 6)

Whether or not you bowl at John Snow's pace, a follow-through is an essential part of delivering the ball (see Chapter 6)

An inspiration to his team! Alan Knott certainly is ... and every young 'keeper should follow his example. Here his general alertness is reflected in an attempt to stump Ian Chappell. The slip fielder is Peter Parfitt (see Chapter 11)

Peter Parfitt plunges to catch Bob Massie in the Third Test between England and Australia in 1972. To reach low snicks like this one, the slip fielder must always crouch down as the ball is delivered by the bowler (see Chapter 10)

Spin Bowling 81

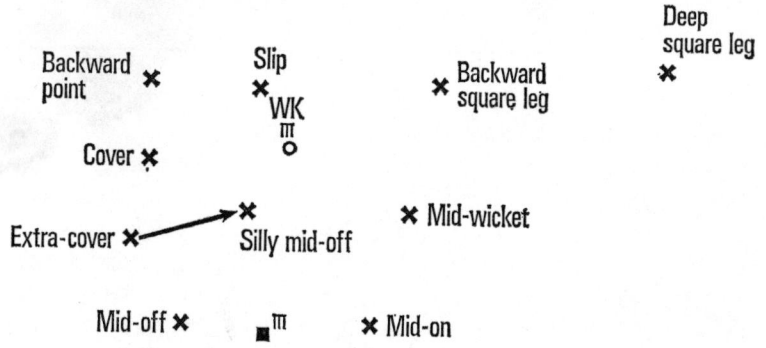

```
Backward                 Slip                                    Deep
point    ✗              ✗                    ✗ Backward          square leg
                         WK                    square leg        ✗
                         ▥
    Cover ✗              ○

                        ➤✗              ✗ Mid-wicket
Extra-cover ✗ ─────    Silly mid-off


Mid-off ✗         ▪▥       ✗ Mid-on
```

Fig. 5. Field for slow left-arm bowler on a good wicket

pitch that much wider of the off stump to hit the wickets or if your standard ball that pitches on the off stump is spinning back so much that it is beating the leg stick, then the answer is to switch to bowling round the wicket. I like to see off spinners operating in this way because it really does change the angle of your delivery. Now with the same amount of turn you have only to pitch just outside the off stump to be sure of hitting middle. In 1956 the legendary Jim Laker, on a turning track at Old Trafford, Manchester, did just this and his bag of 19 wickets in that Test against Australia was a fair testimony to the success of the move.

For the slow left-arm orthodox spinner, the grip and the delivery pattern are just the same as those of the off spinner, except in reverse. The first finger again does all the work, but the ball is spun from right to left, anti-clockwise. The

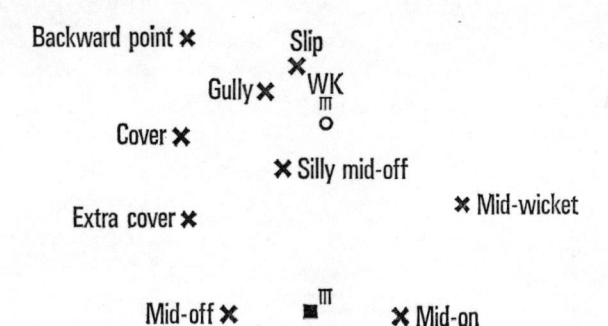

```
       Backward point ✗         Slip
                               ✗
                      Gully ✗   WK
                                ▥
           Cover ✗              ○

                          ✗ Silly mid-off
                                              ✗ Mid-wicket
        Extra cover ✗


               Mid-off ✗    ▪▥    ✗ Mid-on
```

Fig. 6. Field for slow left-arm leg spin on a turning wicket

best line for the left-armer turning the ball towards the slips is around middle and off stumps; here the batsman is compelled to play a shot, and if the ball turns he may well snick a catch. If it doesn't bite into the pitch and spin away, it will still hit the stumps if the batsman misses.

The leg spinner is, perhaps, one of the most controversial bowlers in first class cricket. Wrist spin is difficult to bowl so that there are not many players about who bowl it anyway. It is also difficult to control so that by and large bowlers of this type are expensive, even when they are taking wickets. Consequently, and often quite rightly, captains are not prepared to give their leg-spinner a bowl unless the circumstances are entirely right and he has a lot of runs to play with. At Hampshire there was a very promising leg-spinner called Alan Castell, who eventually gave up his spinning skills to become a medium pace bowler because he got so little bowling. Greg Chappell is another who has foresaken leg break bowling for seam up stuff, and he has since seen more of the ball.

Nevertheless, the top-class leg spinner, like Benaud or the Pakistan Test captain Intikhab Alam or his fellow countryman Mushtaq Mohammad, possesses the ability to bowl a side out. Obviously now there is a scarcity value in their bowling and many players, particularly in England, do not encounter the type often enough to be good at playing them. But more than this, the leg spinner can extract bounce and a considerable amount of turn, and dangerous turn away from the bat at that, from most pitches; the range of deliveries in his potential repertoire can be devastating. At school or club levels, the leg spinner, even without the added weapons of the googly, the top-spinner or the in floater, can be equally destructive. Batting against leg spin bowling is an art that does only come from practice and so few players get the necessary exposure to leg spin in their own nets.

So if you are hoping to be a successful leg spin bowler and you cannot find many to watch in first class cricket, don't be discouraged. Persevere and work hard for that elusive accuracy; you may well get some stick but I promise you that you will pick up enough wickets to compensate.

For the leg break, again grip the ball with the seam across

Spin Bowling

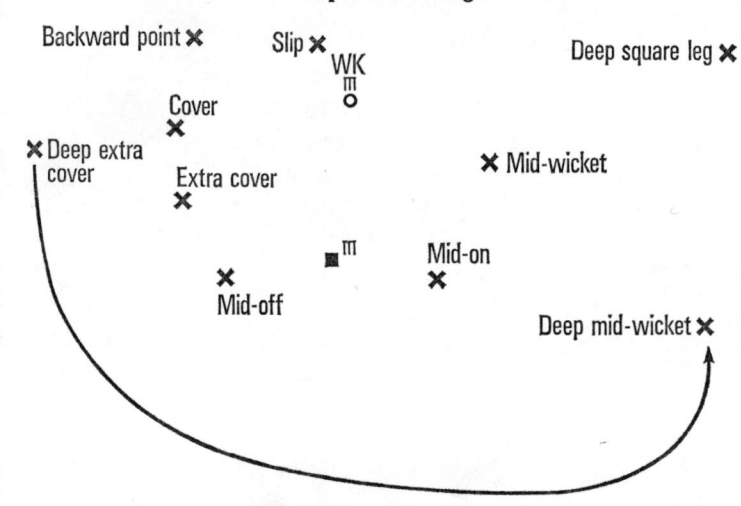

```
Backward point ✘      Slip ✘
                          WK
         Cover           m
            ✘            o
✘ Deep extra
  cover       Extra cover              ✘ Mid-wicket
                  ✘

                        ▪ m    Mid-on
                     ✘         ✘
                     Mid-off
                                   Deep mid-wicket ✘
```

Fig. 7. Field for right-arm leg spin on a good wicket. Place the fielder either at deep extra-cover or deep mid-wicket according to each batsman's preference for shots

the first two fingers. But do not spread the fingers as wide apart as you would do for the off break. Grip with the thumb on the seam on the left hand side, but the finger that actually imparts the spin is now the third finger. As you hold the ball up in front of you, position the third finger against the seam so that it can push the ball into an anti-clockwise spin.

Whereas with the off break the ball comes completely out of the front of the hand and is spun entirely by the fingers, the extra spin and bounce that can be imparted to a leg break come from using the wrist. So instead of showing the batsman the front of the ball as you would do when bowling an off break, bend your wrist back so that the fingers, now pointing towards the leg side, are masking his view of the ball. As you release the ball your wrist also moves in a slightly anti-clockwise direction to give that added thrust to the spin.

The grips for the top spinner and the googly are the same; the difference occurs in the position the ball leaves the hand. For the top spinner – the ball that pitches and goes straight through, but gathers pace off the wicket – really flip the wrist so that the ball comes out not spinning anti-clockwise or clockwise but twisting over and over directly towards the batsman.

Before you try it out in the nets, go out in the garden with a friend and bowl to each other until you are really 'flipping' the ball. A good test to see whether you are imparting the top spin is to watch to see whether the ball dips before pitching, which it will do if you spin it correctly.

The googly, perhaps the better known leg spinners' alternative delivery, is the ball which looks to the batsman just like another leg break but which is in fact an off break and spins back into him. The difference, which you must try to conceal from the striker as much as possible, is that you deliver the googly from out of the back of the hand; this reverses the spin. Whereas you bring the leg break out of the side of your hand, the wrist is almost doubled back for the 'wrong un'. You might find it difficult to begin with to make the googly turn; it may just go through without turning either way. Don't be despondent because this in itself can be an added weapon; the unwary batsman will still be looking for the leg spin, so a straight ball might well sneak through between bat and pad.

The ideal line for a leg spinner must cater for being able to bowl a googly or a 'flipper' and still to take a wicket. I like to see a young leg break bowler pitching on the off stump, because the majority of his wickets are going to come from stumpings and catches in the slips or gully off the edge. If you pitch off stump, the batsman must play a shot or risk being bowled by a delivery that doesn't turn. Once you stray to the leg side the batsman can take a free swing because he can't be out l.b.w. to anything that pitches outside leg stump. On the other hand don't bowl too far outside the off stump because he can then let the ball pass through to the 'keeper with complete safety.

Pitching off stump gives maximum scope to your other deliveries. The googly can nip in and catch the legs in front, so can the top spinner, which should go on to hit the off stump. On this line you are operating at maximum efficiency because all three of your basic deliveries are likely to take a wicket.

To add further subtlety to your bowling as a spinner, you should try to cultivate a change of pace. A quicker delivery

Spin Bowling

can be very effective because most players allow themselves a higher backlift when facing the slower bowlers and if you can slip in a much faster ball, you always have the chance of getting one through before he brings down the bat. For this reason, I am convinced that you should bowl the faster ball as a yorker, particularly if you are an off spinner. I don't like to see a quicker ball pitched on a normal length because I think most competent players can adjust to that, but if you can drive it up into the block hole, you are really bowling a very attacking delivery.

The slower ball, too, deserves careful attention. Try to drop it a little shorter than the normal delivery, but not so short that the batsman can go on to the back foot and pull you through midwicket. The secret is to toss it up just a little higher than normal because almost invariably this draws the batsman forward; he feels sure that he has time to go down the wicket to get to the pitch or to hammer the ball away on the full. Now if you can make it drop around eighteen inches short of where he thinks it is going to land you will upset his calulations.

So whether you are an off spinner or a 'legger', you can become a most proficient bowler by being able to control your stock delivery which pitches around off stump, your quicker ball of yorker length and a slower ball which drops several inches short of the stock ball. For the leg spinner, the slower ball is especially significant because a batsman must be right to the pitch of a leg break to keep his drive along the ground. If he is not there and goes through with his shot the ball must go in the air and the slower ball is designed to do just this, to make him think he is at the pitch when in fact he is a couple of feet short.

Whereas the off spinner might bowl round the wicket when the ball is turning – or to left-handers to avoid the dangers of pitching outside their leg stump – there is not such a great case for leg-spinners to go around the wicket. They might decide to left-handers, but generally to right-handed players the ball is almost certainly going to pitch outside leg. The only real reason you might have for trying it brings us back to Richie Benaud who won Australia the

Old Trafford Test Match of 1961 by doing just this. The other Australian bowlers had dug great pits of footmarks at one end, and Benaud went round the wicket to pitch in these holes. This made the ball lift and turn at differing heights and levels, and the England batsmen, who at the start were chasing victory, just could not cope.

The only other justification for such a move is when, perhaps, you are struggling to break a difficult partnership and you are willing to try anything to give you a little variety. Then you might bowl almost alternately from either side, slipping in one ball from 23 yards, one from wide of the crease, a round-arm slinger, in fact anything to try to catch the batsman out.

But whatever you bowl, you must try to keep the ball well pitched-up. If you drop short and let the batsman go on to the back foot, all your skill is wasted; he can watch the ball bounce, assess its movement and have plenty of time to select which shot to play. Any doubt about a leg break or a googly is immediately resolved without any threat to his wicket.

If there seems to be a great deal to remember, I can assure you that nobody has become a top class spin bowler overnight. The likes of Benaud, Laker and Hugh Tayfield would be the first to admit that they continued to learn throughout their careers. As a spin bowler you can look forward to playing the game for a very long time, so don't try to bite off too much at once.

But this is not to say that you must not put in those hours in the nets. Perhaps as a leg spinner, you need to practise more than any other type of bowler, especially if your own skipper is reluctant to bowl you out there in the middle. But one word of warning; your spinning finger is the tool of your trade so look after it. Don't keep practising until it is red and sore. If it begins to irritate in the nets stop bowling, put some cream on it and rest it. It is a problem that I have rarely suffered with, because my off-spinners are only occasionally summoned into the Hampshire or Natal attack, but I have seen some very worn top joints. However, if you look after it when you are young you are far less likely to have trouble with your spinning finger when you are older.

CHAPTER NINE

Wicket Taking

As a schoolboy cricketer, the secret of consistent bowling success is to attack the stumps. But you will graduate from being the sort of bowler who regularly picks up one or two wickets into the four or five class if you can learn to spot weaknesses in your opponents.

In first class cricket, most bowlers know their adversaries of old and have a good idea of how they can get them out; even if they haven't bowled to a particular batsman before, almost certainly a team-mate with wider experience will offer some advice. At school, you will, of course, not have this advantage, though do try to file away in the back of your mind relevant information on the styles of any player you are likely to encounter again. However, there are certain clues you can pick up as soon as you first set eyes on any batsman.

Take a look at his grip, for a start. If he holds the bat with the back of the top hand facing you, he is likely to be a strong off-side player. So you might begin by bowling him a yorker on his leg stump. If the top hand is further round, the chances are that he will be looking to hit the ball on the leg-side. Therefore it is probably worth probing at him around off stump.

If you are not opening the bowling, but expect to get on soon, watch very closely the batsman that you are soon going to try to dismiss. From every ball that they have to play you should be able to learn something that will help you when you come on. Have a look to see if there is a gap between bat and pad; if you spot that, you have a vulnerable spot to attack immediately you start to bowl. What about backlift? Does one player pick his bat up in a crooked fashion and tend to play across the line? If so, there is another weakness to exploit.

Watch where your opponent is scoring his runs. You can learn one of two things from this. Either he can play one or two shots so well that you know that you must not feed him a half volley, for example, because he is a tremendous off driver, or he favours a shot, perhaps the pull, but does not play it correctly. Now you know that if you drop short he will look to pull you through mid-wicket, but at the same time you also know that he is likely to miscue and get out because his technique is suspect. In either case, if you haven't been observant, you are going to receive some unnecessary punishment and lose the opportunity of taking a wicket.

If you are a slow bowler, pay particular attention to a player who likes to use his feet. When you come on to have a go at him, you are already armed with this vital piece of information and so you can vary your flight and pace to try to lure him to his doom. Don't worry about getting hit; this is the least of your troubles. Bowl to your field and encourage the batsman by tossing one up now and again; with a little guile you have an excellent chance of inducing a false stroke which he would not make if you continually bowled at the same pace.

When I was at school, I was very lucky because our coach used to umpire, and when I bowled from his end he would give me little tips like 'This fellow's very strong off his toes,' or 'Try this chap with a slower one.' I must admit it was very helpful, but I hoped I was looking to spot these weaknesses myself. If you are a bowler, there is no excuse for loafing about in the field. Keep your eyes open and try to build up this picture of the strengths and weaknesses of each batsman's game.

Once you have done this, try to attack the weaknesses. And sometimes it might pay you to feed a strength. Ali Bacher, the South African skipper, readily admits that he can be tied down by a delivery which appears to be wasted because it is directed at his favourite shots. Ali is very much an on-side player; in fact apart from the cut he very rarely plays on the off side at all. Yet he confesses that the hardest ball for him to score off is the one that pitches on leg stump with a strong leg-side field placed to cut off the stroke. He finds that he has far more room to swing freely – even if it is across the line – when the ball is pitched outside the off stump. So the way to limit Ali Bacher is to bowl to his strength; if you bowl to what appears to be his weakness, around the off stump, he will simply crack you away through mid-on.

Having the correct field to each batsman is another way to increase your wicket-taking potential. Obviously if you are an outswing bowler there is a stock field you will employ, just as there is if you bowl the off break. But these are only guidelines which you will vary depending on the batsman who is facing you. If you are an outswing bowler, you will probably want a six-three field, six men on the off side and three on the leg. But if one player keeps whacking you over midwicket, it's no good saying to yourself that he shouldn't be hitting you there and leaving the field as it is. Put an extra man on the leg side to try to put a stop to his tricks, but don't necessarily leave him there. If the chap at the other end is playing you in a very orthodox manner, then bring the mid-wicket across to the off-side again, as soon as the batsmen change ends. Your field should be set, in discussion with your captain, to counter each batsman's own range of shots.

At Hampshire or in the Currie Cup, whenever we face Mike Procter on a good wicket, we stick a man out on the boundary at deep extra cover because we know that Mike isn't afraid to loft the ball over the off-side field. When Ian Chappell is facing slow bowlers, you will invariably see a deep square leg because he loves to play the sweep. Chris Wilkins of Border and Derbyshire loves to hit the ball over mid-on, and so on a good wicket most fielding sides will send someone down to the long-on boundary as soon as he comes into bat.

But if the wicket is slightly in the bowler's favour, it can be more profitable to leave gaps to encourage the batsman to play a shot that might get him out providing that the ball 'does a bit'. There was no happier example of this for me than in an Eastern Province versus Natal clash that decided the fate of the Currie Cup a few seasons back. Eastern Province needed two hundred odd in the last innings to win the match and were about 150 for 3 or 4 when Jackie McGlew brought on Trevor Goddard to bowl. Eddie Barlow was going great guns, and if Natal were to stand any chance they had to get him out quickly.

If you have ever seen Barlow bat, you will know that he loves to play the cut, and he must have been pleasantly surprised when he saw the off-side field McGlew set with Goddard – a slip, a backward point and extra cover and a deep mid-off. No one at cover-point. It was a gap that Barlow could not resist. He went for his favourite square cut, but the ball nipped back at him off the wearing last-day wicket. It scraped the under-edge of his bat and hit the stumps. Eastern Province collapsed, lost the game and Natal took the Currie Cup.

As well as consulting with your captain on field placings, you should also discuss which end you should bowl. Sometimes, of course, you will not have the choice, but whenever possible try to utilise the conditions to your advantage. If you are a quick bowler, obviously you will be happier with the wind at your back rather than having to battle into the teeth of a gale. If there is a cross breeze, try to get on at the end which helps your natural swing; if you bowl in-swingers, for example, you will want to have the cross wind coming from left to right.

As a slow bowler it is more advisable to bowl into the wind. Most spinners prefer this because when the ball is tossed up the wind will hold it up even more. Down wind, a highly flighted delivery can easily end up as a friendly full pitch. Derek Underwood often prefers to bowl with the wind, but he is of the quicker variety of spinner who relies on changes of pace rather than consistent use of flight. Another way a spin bowler can use conditions to suit him is if there is any slope across the wicket. At a ground like Lord's where

Wicket Taking

there is a slope towards the Tavern, most off spinners prefer to bowl from the pavilion end because the angle of the ground tends to pull the ball in the direction they are trying to spin. Conversely, leg spinners and slow left-armers by and large prefer the Nursery End.

It is important, too, to make adjustments in line and length according to the pace of the pitch. As a quickie on a fast track, you can probably pitch a little short of a length, knowing that the ball will lift and fly through, almost certainly at a height that will disconcert the batsman. But if you do this on a slow, dead pitch or a wet wicket with no bounce, you will give any player so much time to get on to the back foot that he will hit you to all parts of the ground. On the other hand, if there is a little movement in the pitch for seamers or cutters, you might pitch just short of a good length where the batsman cannot smother the deviation by playing right forward.

Making use of the conditions is one of the signs of being a good bowler. If you are an off spinner and you are playing on a 'turner', your side will be looking to you to bowl the opposition out. But don't think it will be easy. Most top-class bowlers will tell you that it is a problem adjusting to favourable conditions. The ball might turn too much, for example, and so you are not forcing the batsmen to play many balls. You will find that you have to concentrate every bit as much as you do when bowling on a plumb pitch.

Basically unless the batsman is in trouble on the back foot, always try to bring him forward. Length and line on a good wicket, pitching around the off stump, should keep you in with a chance of a wicket when the odds seem to be stacked in favour of the batsman.

Remember, too, that as a bowler, you are some sort of an athlete. You must look after yourself, particularly if you are a fast bowler. In county dressing-rooms you will always find quick bowlers spending ten minutes doing limbering-up exercises before the beginning of an innings or a session of play in which they are starting the bowling. If you run up and bowl cold, there is every chance that a muscle, that is far from ready for the strenuous exercise involved in bowling, will tear. And there is nothing worse than spending a month on and off the treatment table whilst all your mates are having the fun of playing.

In this respect the captain must play his part. He should always try to give his bowlers a couple of overs notice that they are going to be called upon, so that they can begin to limber up in the field, stretching every muscle that comes into play as they run up, bringing their arms over and following through. To keep the muscles warm in between overs, don't be afraid to resort to a sweater, even though at the end of one over you may have sweat dripping off you. In the three or four minutes before you are on again you could catch cold or pick up a summer chill. It is just not worth the risk. In South Africa or Australia, a sleeveless sweater will do fine, but since the average English summer's day is much like midwinter in Durban, I would advise most fast bowlers to go on to the field with a long-sleeved pullover and probably a sleeveless underneath that. Preparation of this kind should never be neglected. After all, it's very difficult taking wickets from the masseur's room.

Whilst on the subject of anatomy, there is one final place where a bowler must be strong – in his heart. Cricket can be the most frustrating of games, and the bowler has to bear his share of disappointments. One afternoon you may really hit top form, yet still walk off the field with nought for sixty because four or five catches have been put down. Another day you may deservedly end up with the same figures because you haven't bowled well. These are the times when you need your heart, and a belief in yourself. Just as in batting, you will experience bad patches, and as a bowler you might experience them, as I have said, simply because your fielders aren't doing their job. But you will never fight back if you allow yourself to become despondent. Show the strength of your character by working harder and harder and sticking to your task until the tide turns, as it inevitably will.

You can learn so much from looking at the great bowlers, at their style and techniques. But look deeper and you will see their resilience and persistence. That is one quality of bowling you can directly copy.

CHAPTER TEN

The Techniques of Fielding

When I am coaching young players I so often find that they are only really interested in being at the centre of the action – that is, either batting or bowling. Fielding is regarded as no more than a chore which must be endured to be able to do these more exciting things. But this is perhaps one of the most unhealthy attitudes a young cricketer can have and to make the grade it is one that must be dismissed.

Fielding is so important. It can be the make or break of a side. Not only will the dropping or holding of catches determine the course of a game, but if your side works at ground fielding numerous runs can be saved. Moreover, as a member of the team, your chances of keeping your place during a bad run with bat or ball will be much greater if you contribute athletically in the field.

In this respect, I think you will benefit if you try to become a specialist in one position. Obviously you must achieve a reasonable standard anywhere in the field because circumstances might dictate that there is no need for you to remain throughout an innings in the position of your choice. Yet if you favour fielding at short leg or gully or somewhere in the deep, give this aspect of your cricket as much consideration and attention as you would to your batting or bowling.

At school, I was never the quickest thing on two legs, so I decided that I was going to have to prove that I could catch close to the wicket better than the others in order to show my worth in the field. So I concentrated on becoming a specialist slip. That early practice paid off because when I first played top-class cricket at home there were so many good 'slippers' that I really had to catch everything that came my way to earn the right to stay there.

The golden rules about slip fielding are: to bend low as the bowler runs in and to stay down until the batsman has played his shot. Then you will be in position if a low snick comes to you. It is much easier to move up rather than down, so you are also well prepared for the chance which flies higher.

Most of my time is spent at first slip, and from here you should watch the ball all the way from the bowler's hand. Position yourself a yard or so behind the 'keeper when he is standing back, but how fine you stand really depends on the stumper's skill. In Natal we have Denis Gamsy behind the stumps; he is a soccer goalkeeper and can cover a lot of ground, so I stand a little wider. As a first slip, your relationship with the 'keeper is crucial, so bear in mind how far he is likely to come across in front of you.

These problems increase with the 'keeper standing up. Naturally how deep you stand depends on the speed of the bowling and how far a snick will carry. To a medium pacer like Trevor Jesty at Hampshire, 'keeper Bob Stephenson goes up to the stumps and I stand about eight or ten yards back. In this situation I think you must take up a fine position because the 'keeper cannot adjust to cover so many little nicks. For the slow left-armer, stand much closer and a little wider.

At second slip your position is obviously dictated by where first slip is standing. You must ensure that a snick cannot pass between the two of you, but at the same time you must cover the maximum possible area. If you both stretch out an arm so that your fingers touch, you are round about the right spot. From second slip you have an option about watching the ball on to the bat or simply electing to focus your eyes on the outside edge. This really is a matter of choice. In first-class cricket, Ian Chappell, and Graham Roope, regularly a top catcher in county cricket, prefer to

The Techniques of Fielding

watch the ball the whole way; others pay attention to the bat only.

But in the gully, there is no question about it. Because you are much squarer to the batsman, you must watch the bat. This applies whether you are fielding in the deep gully position – where you are hoping to catch the ball off the meat of the bat or a thick outside edge – or if you are brought in closer for the ball that pops and hits the splice or the one that comes off the inside edge and across off the pad.

At gully and at short leg, it is not easy to define how close you should stand because the ball is likely to come in your direction at such a variety of paces. Eventually from experience, you will cultivate an instinct for how far back to go to each of your team's bowlers. At short leg, you must also concentrate on watching the bat and picking up your sight of the ball from there when it comes your way.

At short leg always wear a protector. Not only will it save you from the risk of a most painful blow, but it will give you the confidence to face the batsman. So many short legs automatically turn away as soon as the batsman shapes to play the ball on the leg side. Obviously there are times when evasive action must be taken, but it can be very infuriating when a sweep is played, for example, and the ball strikes the gloves and dollies up only to be missed by a short leg who has turned his back too soon.

On top of this, a courageous close fielder can unsettle and distract a batsman. I shall never forget the first time I played against Brian Close when he was with Yorkshire. On a drying wicket at Harrogate in my initial season with Hampshire, he stood so close that I could touch his leg. His unflinching courage certainly made his presence felt. I remember thinking that if I made one mistake playing on the leg side, even if it was off an attacking shot, this chap would face up and try to catch it.

You will also need to be brave if you want to specialise as a close fielder in front of the bat. Here you have no alternative but to watch the bat because you would have to twist 180 degrees to follow the ball from the bowler's hand. Try to keep as low as possible, both to avoid being hit and to pick up the boot high chances. Remember that most high catches will probably carry to mid-on or mid-off. Stand as close as you can without impairing your judgement. It may look brave to be two yards from the bat, but you are not doing your job if you are so near that you have no chance of adjusting when the ball is played in the air.

For all these close positions, there is a basic catching technique, which I feel gives you the maximum opportunity of hanging on to what comes your way. Always use two hands whenever you can and keep them close together. If the catch comes around waist height or below, point your fingers down and slightly towards the direction from which the ball is coming. Your two little fingers should be together and the hands should form a slight cup.

As the ball comes towards you, try to get your eyes in line with its flight so that you can spot any swerving through the air. Hold your hands slightly in front of your body, which can act as a back stop if the ball slips through; this might give you a second chance to make the catch. As it strikes your hands, relax them slightly so that it doesn't strike a firm surface and bounce away. Try to think of cushioning the impact. Now draw the hands close into the body and wrap your fingers around the ball.

If a catch comes to you higher, reverse this method. Point the fingers upwards, bringing the thumbs together. The technique is then the same, with the emphasis once more on cushioning the impact of ball on hand. Around the waist, there is this sort of grey area in which you might get away with either method. I am a great believer in the below-the-waist technique, because if you misjudge your effort, the chances are that the ball will bounce up from palms or wrists and you might have another bite at it. With the other method you are more likely to knock the ball to the ground.

The only way to tighten up your technique and to give razor edges to your reflexes is to keep in practice. Before the start of a top-class game you will always see the close fielders hitting short catches off a bat to each other in front of the pavilion. Reflexes are soon dulled if you don't work at them. After all, your first chance might not come until you have been in the field for four or five hours; it could be the only one you'll get and you have got to catch it.

Any form of practice will help. You might begin by throwing a tennis ball against a wall and snapping up the rebounds. This will attune you to the speed of a fast-moving ball without bruising your hands. From this you can move on to working on slip-catching machines of various shapes and sizes that most clubs possess. In Natal we add an element of competition to our practice by playing games of six-a-side touch rugby with a hockey ball. This is great fun and it does put you under the sort of pressure that most practice lacks but that is always there when you play a proper match.

All this will help that other vital quality so necessary in a specialist close fielder – concentration. Look at it this way. The bowlers in your team are giving their all to try to induce a snick or any sort of false stroke. At the moment they do that they have succeeded. But if a fraction of a second later you put that catch down, their effort has been wasted. And if you have ever bowled an over in your life you are sure to know how heart-breaking that can become if it happens regularly. Of course catches will go down; no one will expect you to catch everything. But if you are guilty of lack of concentration you will not only upset the bowler, you will also risk being injured.

Of course, the great catch will also lift the bowler and encourage your whole team. If you hang on to a blinder, you are doing your job and more. I will never forget Don Mackay-Coghill of Transvaal picking me up in the gully. I really slashed hard off the back foot and the ball went so fast that it was in his hand before I realised what had happened. He caught it in his left-hand at full stretch, a really remarkable effort and the bowler looked twice the man he had been when he bowled to our next batsman.

At first slip, you can also help by passing on anything you notice to your skipper or bowlers. From there you have a first-class view of any movement off the wicket, or of the pace the ball is coming through. By concentrating you will pick up these bits of information and you may well help indirectly in the taking of wickets.

Often the close catchers capture the limelight because more opportunities to shine acrobatically come their way. But every side needs competent outfielders and you can be just as brilliant and effective away from the bat as you can five yards from the stumps. Remember a run saved equals a run made. If at cover you make five good stops in an afternoon, you have saved twenty runs; if the ball goes through to the fence someone has to go out and make those runs.

Men like Colin Bland in South Africa, Paul Sheahan and Ross Edwards in Australia and Clive Lloyd, the lithe West Indian, save their sides hundreds of runs in a season. In Sheahan's case, his contribution in the field has been so valuable that occasionally it has kept him in the Australian side even though he was struggling for form with the bat. Colin Bland, too, originally owed his selection for South Africa to his brilliance in the outfield.

Outfielding, too, requires concentration, although of a less intense form. Here you must always be on your toes, literally. Make a small mark at the place in the field where the captain wants you, then walk back a few yards. As the bowler runs in, you move in as well, so that you reach the mark as the batsman plays the ball. Because you are already on the move, you will react much quicker to the needs of the situation. Most run-outs are by a matter of inches, and you are trying to make those inches by your speed and agility. But don't become so concerned that you stray past that mark; that is where you were put, so that is where you should be. You are likely to receive a deserving lecture if a catch drops just behind you or a ball whistles past you for four because you have come in five yards too close.

When you field the ball, use the barrier method, covering a two-handed pick up with your knee. A well-struck drive might burst through your hands, but you will save the runs if your leg is behind the line. One-handed pick-ups are more spectacular, but much less reliable, and you really should be absolutely proficient in practice before you attempt it in the match. Again consider your bowler; he'll not be at all happy if you come sweeping in and miss the ball completely.

The Techniques of Fielding

Try always when you pick up one-handed to place one foot behind the ball as a second line of defence.

At a very last resort you might try to make a diving stop or use your feet. I am not really a fan of either method. The result could easily be an injury – a grass burn or a pulled muscle from the dive or a twisted ankle from treading on the ball – which could end your contribution to the game and put you on the sidelines for a few weeks.

Once you have collected the ball the next task is to return it to the 'keeper as quickly as possible. Throwing comes naturally to some young players but others, who perhaps are in the process of outgrowing their strength, find it a little harder. I am a great believer in the overarm technique. As you start to throw, hold the other arm out in front of you, as though you were pointing to the wicket-keeper and then propel the ball forward with a bent arm almost in the bowling position.

If you naturally throw with a 'flat' or side-arm action, take a little extra care in your aim because you are letting go of the ball away from your body and your eyes are not in the perfect position to line up the target. With either method you must try to reach the 'keeper on the full, with as low a trajectory as your strength allows. The flatter the throw, the less time it takes to reach the target.

If you find that you are too far away to be sure that you can reach on the full, don't try it. I have seen a lot of youngsters dangling a limp arm because they have overstrained themselves. I have also come across several 'keepers with injured fingers because they have had to pick up awkward throws that arrive on the half volley or bounce just in front of them. If you know that you are not going to reach, try to bounce the ball about fifteen yards short so that it arrives at a catchable height. The 'keeper should always be your target because, after all, he is the man with the protected hands. The only exceptions to this rule should be either when you are going for a run-out at the bowler's end or when you are throwing in from the boundaries behind the bowler. Even then if you can reach the 'keeper in the distance, do so.

Always stay alert. It is not always easy to keep your mind on the job during a long stint in the field, but it will help if you look for weaknesses in the running between the wickets of your opponents. If you spot any uncertainty look to capitalise on it. You must also be alert to the needs of backing-up, covering a team-mate as you would like to have one covering you if you misfield. Be ready to take returns at the bowlers' ends to protect their hands.

All aspects of groundfielding, catching in the deep and throwing must come into your practices. Go back to the example of Colin Bland. His throwing practices, where he could time and time again knock out one stump from twenty yards, became legendary. Fans came just to watch him at these sessions. His patience paid off, too; he turned himself into probably the greatest fielder of all-time. His dedication should be an inspiration to you.

The most usual practice for catching and throwing as a team involves the fielders encircling a player with a bat and the 'keeper standing by one stump. The ball is driven to someone in the ring and he has to catch it or field it cleanly and then hurl it in over the stump. If this becomes tedious turn it into a competition giving marks for catches held and accurate throwing. It soon adds an edge to the proceedings.

If you ever find being in the field a chore, just take a good look at the game you are playing. Whether you are batsman or bowler, you are still a fielder, and your ability as a cricketer will be judged according to how well you can perform in this role. Fielding is just as exciting and stimulating as batting and bowling. You will never find it dull if you are holding catches and saving runs.

CHAPTER ELEVEN

Wicket-Keeping

The 'keeper is the most specialised fielder of all. Always in the action, his job is vitally important to the side at all levels of the game. There are so many facets of the task. He must be able to hang on to the catching and stumping chances which will inevitably come his way; he must be sufficiently agile to keep the number of extras down to a minimum; he must be shrewd enough to advise his bowlers and captain on any aspect of the way the pitch is playing; and above all his general standard of alertness must be an inspiration to his team-mates in the field.

I was fortunate enough to be able to appreciate the demands made on a 'keeper when I came over to England with the South African Schools' side in 1963. We had two 'keepers, but on the odd occasion that both needed a rest or one was just played for his batting, I took the gloves. I really enjoyed the opportunity because behind the stumps you are always in the game. The problem for me was that I felt that if I had taken up the job seriously it would have slowly undermined my effectiveness as a batsman. I fully believe that if you are a 'keeper, your first responsibility is to become a specialist behind the stumps. If you happen to be a useful batsman, don't neglect your natural skills. But at the same time you must never allow your batting to push your 'keeping into the background.

There have been several batsman-keepers, as opposed to

'keepers who can bat, perhaps the most notable of whom was Jim Parks of Sussex and England. Parks did a fair job for his country, especially with the bat, but I always felt that the selectors had made the wrong approach. For me the best 'keeper, irrespective of whether he knew which end of the bat to hold, would always be the first choice in a Test or county match. In the limited-overs competitions, there is perhaps more need for a 'keeper who can contribute his share of the runs.

Study and practice of the correct techniques will improve your work behind the wicket. Obviously the most basic of these is the correct method of taking the ball. Without this aptitude, whatever other talents you possess, you will always be struggling to do the job properly. The only real way to ensure that the ball regularly sticks to your gloves is to extend the catching method that we discussed when talking about slip-fielding. Keep the little fingers closely pressed together and the fingers pointing downwards. So many young 'keepers begin by catching the ball with one hand on top of the other, like an alligator swallowing a fly, but this can be very painful. If you misjudge the pace of the ball, it can easily strike you full on the ends of the fingers and possibly break a bone.

So keep the hands side-by-side and cupped. Because you are wearing gloves, you must ensure even more that your hands give on contact. The thick palms of the gauntlets will not cushion the ball on their own, so let your hands ride into your body. This will absorb the pace and keep the ball in the gloves. This should not be an extravagant movement, but just a gentle 'give' of a few inches. If you get the chance, take a look at someone like Alan Knott from the square leg boundary and you will see how he brings the ball into his body.

Practise this until it becomes second nature, until it almost becomes impossible for you to take the ball any other way. Take a friend out into the park with you and simply ask him to throw you the ball, and especially to bounce it a few yards in front of you so that it comes through at the sort of height you will have to take deliveries in a match.

Wicket-Keeping

Those gloves must become as much a part of you as the skin on your hands.

As with batting, you will find it very much easier to make contact with the ball if your eyes are behind and as level as possible with the line of flight. This is why you always see 'keepers crouch as the bowler runs in. By going down, your eyes are on a line parallel with the bounce of the ball, and you should only straighten up at the very last moment. So many youngsters straighten up too soon and miss the ball because it has come through too low. I think that if you understand the logic behind going down – because it puts you in the perfect position to judge the height of the bounce – you will avoid having this fault in your own game.

Bend down into a squatting position whether you are standing back or up at the stumps. Some 'keepers prefer to keep their hands outside their pads, but I like to see them held inside, ready and waiting in the cupped position. This is Alan Knott's style and he is the best 'keeper I have ever seen; so what is good enough for him is definitely good enough for you. Whilst you are down, keep balanced on the balls of your feet so that when it is time to come up, or when you have to dart down the leg-side, you are perfectly balanced to do so quickly.

Standing back is obviously the easier of the two roles. You have much more time to see the ball and to adjust your position to meet it, whether it comes straight through or off the pads or the bat. Make a mark with your left foot level with the off stump so that you have an unhindered view of the ball. How far you stand back will depend on the pace of both bowler and pitch, but there is a simple guideline. Take up your stance where the ball is just reaching the top of its arc after it has bounced. If it is coming down by the time it arrives in your gloves, move forward; if you are regularly being struck on the chest, retreat a pace or two.

As you take the ball, straighten up and bring your legs together. The pads form a very useful second line of defence, but, and I do stress this, they must only be used in emergencies. A 'keeper who continually relies on his pads will not only look shoddy when he should be trying to be neat but will also kick away unnecessary byes. Always have the pads behind your gloves to act as back stop in case the ball wriggles through, but they should never be your first line of defence.

When the ball flies down the leg-side, it will not always be possible to bring the pads into line, so you must concentrate on bringing the hands into the correct position. You should be able to reach a large percentage of these deliveries by taking two or three nimble steps to your left, but if you know you are going to fall short, the last resort is to dive. This is fine as long as it is understood that you do stand a far better chance of clinging on to the ball if you don't dive. I'm afraid that as a coach I do note a tendency for young players to go for the spectacular for its own sake – in this case probably because they have seen someone like Denis Lindsay or Alan Knott take a blinding leg-side catch at full stretch. You can be certain that these great 'keepers prefer to reach the ball without that athletic plunge. It can easily bounce out of the gloves if an elbow or shoulder jars against the ground.

Standing up to the stumps to slow or medium pace bowling is an even greater test of your ability, and most of the top-class 'keepers make their mistakes up at the wicket. Here your bravery is put to the test because there is a much greater risk of you taking a knock, but if you are positive in your actions and sound in your catching technique, there is no reason why you should not be able to reach a competent standard. Perhaps the biggest failing is for the reason that I have touched on already. Because there is less time to move up from the crouch position, young 'keepers tend to stand up as soon as the bowler has delivered the ball. If you can discipline yourself not to straighten until the bounce, you will find that suddenly you are in the right place to make the take, as the ball comes to you on the rise.

If you go bolt upright too soon, you will find it particularly hard to move across to make leg-side takes. If you make it across in time, the ball will glance off your pads for almost certain byes, but more often you won't be there

Wicket-Keeping

at all and can only throw a despairing hand at the ball. So don't move at all upwards or sideways until you are quite sure of the line and bounce of each delivery.

Standing up does mean exactly that. Because there is a considerable temptation to try to gain an extra half second to make a clean take, young 'keepers are inclined to move back away from the wickets. Unless you are long in the arm, you should never stand more than 12 to 15 inches from the stumps. Further back and there will be no way you can reach forward to make a stumping from that position. There really is no 'in-between' position. Either you stand back or you are right up close.

In making a stumping you should try to be as neat as in any of your work. To break the wicket you only have to remove one bail; you are awarded nothing extra for scything down all three sticks. Obviously if you have to dive to knock down the stumps to make a run-out, you are concerned with simply making contact of any sort. But when you are close to the stumps, one bail will do. It makes you look a tidy 'keeper and it does show how much you are in control over your movements.

With so much emphasis on co-ordination and concentration, it is imperative that whenever you go to the nets you practise your 'keeping. It may be very tempting for you to pick up the ball and fool around with your bowling. This really is a waste of time, and apart from perhaps a net with the bat, you should have your gloves on all the time.

If you have a slow and a fast practice net, you can stand behind the stumps in the slow one and enjoy an intense workout. If the nets are of mixed pace, I think you are better advised to avoid any risk of injury by practising outside. Take a team-mate, one stump and a ball and find yourself some space. Ask him to bowl so that you have to take a whole variety of deliveries standing up at the stump. If you can persuade another friend to stand in as a batsman so much the better. He should shape to play the ball and then at the last minute let it go through for you to take.

You will also be involved in the outfielding practices for the rest of the team and here you must encourage them to throw over the top of the stumps. Your enthusiasm will help lift the others and it will do no harm if you have a playful moan at them when they throw badly. If they know you are doing your best to help make their throwing look good, they will do their best to help you.

Out in the middle your view of what is happening delivery by delivery is second to none, so you must be mentally as well as physically alert. Your relationship with the bowlers should produce wickets for the side. You might spot that one player topples over when he plays the ball on the leg side. He becomes a likely candidate for a leg-side stumping. The bowler might not have spotted this but if you tell him to slip in a quick ball outside the leg stump second ball of his next over, you can be sharply into position to attempt the stumping. In a less specific way, you can advise the skipper about the pace of the pitch. He might have set two slips on a track that turns out to be slower than expected; you might then suggest that the second slip becomes a second gully.

You are a central figure all the time your side is fielding and you must work at your game to justify such a position. A good fielding side can be made to look quite moderate by an indifferent 'keeper, but the neat stumper can really lift an average set of fielders.

CHAPTER TWELVE

The Responsibilities of the Skipper

As a youngster I shall never forget the kindness shown to Mike Procter and myself when we both began our first class careers. Jackie McGlew, then the Natal skipper, helped all he could to make us relax and acclimatise to the higher demands of the game. I think both Mike and I adjusted much more quickly to these new pressures because of Jackie's guidance.

To me this was a fine example of good captaincy. The key to being a success in this role is to be able to regularly produce the best from each member of your side. Much of this work takes place on the field, but in this case Jackie's consideration off the field undoubtedly helped us to settle in and make scores much sooner than we otherwise would have done.

Captains ripen and mature with experience, but as a skipper of a school side there are many aspects of the job you can learn right from the start of your career. Because so much of your active leadership takes place whilst you are fielding, you can begin by studying all the fielding positions so that you know them off by heart. Most of them you will probably know already, but you can look at them in a new light by trying to decide which of your team are likely to be suited to each position and what combinations of positions you will require for each of your bowlers.

When you are in the field, set your fielders in consultation with the bowler, with some clear idea of how you are going to try to dismiss each batsman. You must work hand in glove with the bowlers. It is no good your setting one field if the bowler has another idea in mind. Between you, you must decide how he is going to attack each opponent, whether he is going to feed a strength or try to undo a weakness.

When you direct the fielders to their positions make sure that they know exactly where they should be standing. With very young players, it might not be enough to tell them to go to mid-wicket or extra cover; they might only have a hazy idea of where that is. Check that every fielder is exactly where you and the bowler want him – moreover make sure that they stay in position. It is easy to wander 15 yards away from where you should be. Encourage all your team to make a mark to keep them where they are supposed to stand.

At the end of each over, it is a test of your organising ability to make sure that no fielder has to make a long journey to his spot for the other bowler. A trip from third man to third man is enough to try the fitness and the patience of any enthusiast. Sometimes, of course, a longish switch will be unavoidable, but in the main encourage a smooth changeover. As you establish a regular side, your fielders should know where they are required to be as soon as they see who is about to bowl. Always try to be consistent; never have any lad fielding at slip and long leg alternate matches. Try to cultivate a side of specialists who have the versatility to adapt when required.

The power to change the bowling rests with you and which bowler you bring on is very much determined by the conditions under which you are playing. In school cricket, the usual trend is for the faster bowlers to begin and to be replaced by a couple of spinners, with the speedmen returning for a final fling if required. This is sound basis, which often happens in first-class cricket, but as skipper you have to learn to be flexible and to assess which of your five or six bowlers is likely to use the conditions to best effect. If the wicket is slow and not turning and your spinners are being hammered, you will have to resort to your quick men again. Or if the seamers are presenting all sorts of problems, they must be kept on longer than you might normally bowl them.

In these situations, your bowlers, the vice-captain and the wicket-keeper should be encouraged to offer any advice. As a captain I have always told my players that they should feel free to suggest any alteration in the field or a change in an approach to a troublesome opponent. This is not to say that three times an over you want players racing up and whispering in your ear, but a quiet word between overs should always be appreciated even if you don't agree with the suggestion.

Discipline on the field is also an integral part of the captain's task. Few cricketers at any level are out-and-out troublemakers on the field. Any problem children usually find themselves quickly without a game, but as skipper you must ensure that concentration is maintained throughout the side. One problem, often rife in school sides, is persistent chattering. Not only does this usually point to a lack of application, it is also extremely discourteous to the opposing batsmen. Talking is perfectly all right at the fall of wicket or even between overs, but only the odd words passed amongst the slips should be spoken during an over. Even then these must cease as the bowler begins his run.

In first-class cricket there are several compulsive talkers, like Peter Parfitt, and if you restrict them you unsettle them; they talk to help themselves concentrate. Yet these are such disciplined players that they never allow a chat to disturb a batsman or unsettle their concentration. At school level, it is probably wiser to limit the talking to between overs.

I am a great admirer of the approach to discipline shown by Ian Chappell when I played for him in South Australia. He felt that his players were all of sufficient experience to know exactly what standards were required of them, and so he imposed few formal rules either on or off the field. Yet you knew that if you infringed these standards, you were likely to receive a pretty severe ticking off.

In all matters of captaincy on the field, you will learn so

much to add to your own experience if you go and watch first-class cricket. I know that at 13 and 14 years old, many youngsters are more concerned with playing their own games behind the boundary ropes rather than watching; and, of course, I would not want to discourage anyone from playing. Nevertheless there is so much to learn from watching.

If you are the skipper of a side, study a top-class skipper in action. Try to understand why he has placed his field in a certain way; why some bowlers have been used but others have not and how he is trying to master the threat of each batsman. Watch him closely to understand his relationship with the fielders; it should only take the flick of a hand or a nod of the head to make an alteration in the field. At many grounds in England and South Africa you are allowed to walk out at the intervals to have a look at the actual batting strip. You can even learn a little from this to build up your library of experience so that eventually you will be able to assess pitches before the game starts.

There are very few moments for the skipper to relax whilst he is fielding, but his responsibilities do not end there. When it is his side's turn to bat, he has to decide on the batting order, although at school this might be agreed jointly with the master-in-charge. The aim with the order is to have each member of the side happy with their position, and all doing well enough to keep it settled week after week. In practice this isn't always possible. If you have four men wanting to open, then two of them are going to be disappointed. If one player has not been too successful at the position of his choice, you might have to persuade him that he would be better off elsewhere.

Whilst the actual batting is taking place, the captain is able to grab a little relaxation and put up his feet. But there may still be little things deserving of his attention. Whilst keeping half-an-eye on how things are progressing in the middle, he may be called upon to do what Jackie McGlew did for Mike Procter and myself. There may be a young lad promoted from the Under-15 side who would welcome and benefit from a few kind words. Another player might have been going through a bad trot and five minutes with him,

The Responsibilities of the Skipper 111

assuring him that his place is not endangered, might really pay off when he takes his turn at the crease.

I have been fortunate in that I have played under some fine skippers. McGlew and Chappell I have already mentioned, and Peter van der Merwe was another. They each had their different ways of doing things, but their common aim was the fostering of team spirit and the good of the side. Bearing that in your mind and cultivating a sense of responsibility, you should find that being asked to lead a team is extremely rewarding.

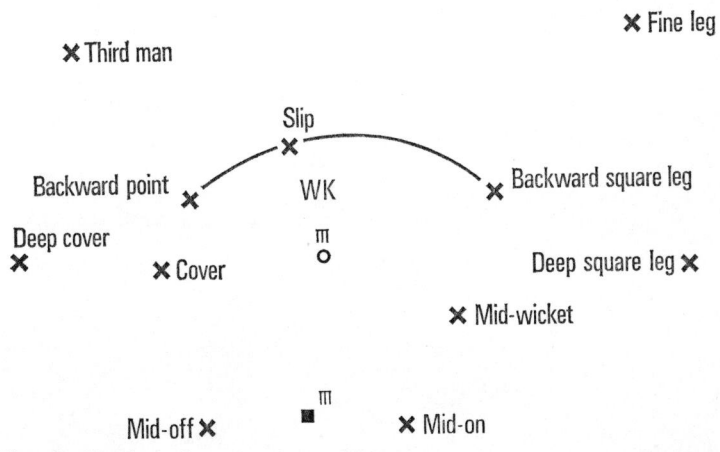

Fig. 8. Typical fast bowler's field for a 60-over limited innings. Depending, of course, on the state of the game, the slip would probably be moved to a more defensive position at backward point or backward square leg

```
        Backward point ✘                    ✘ Backward square leg
                               WK
                               ⊓
  ✘ Deep cover                  ○             Deep square leg ✘
              ✘ Cover
                                          ✘ Mid-wicket


                                 ⊓
       Mid-off ✘         ■      Mid-on
                                  ✘       Deep mid-wicket ✘
           │                       │
           │                       │
           ▼                       ▼                     ↘
```

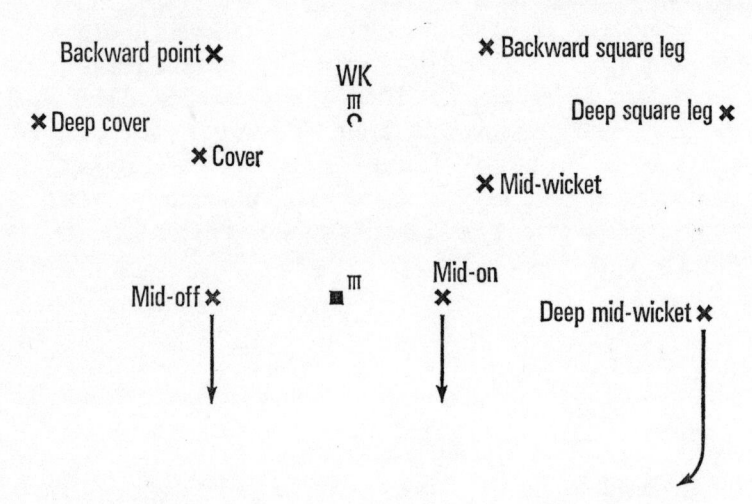

Fig. 9. Typical slow bowler's field for a 60-over limited innings

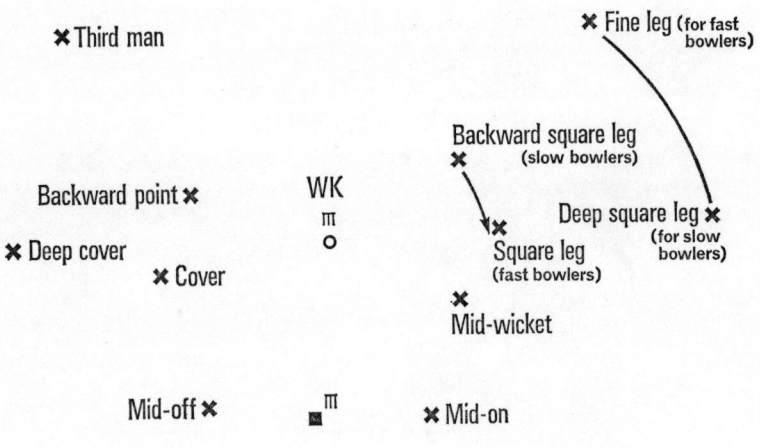

```
                                              ✘ Fine leg (for fast
   ✘ Third man                                              bowlers)

                                       Backward square leg
                                        ✘   (slow bowlers)
                              WK         ✘              (for slow
   Backward point ✘           ⊓        Square leg    Deep square leg ✘
                              ○       (fast bowlers)     bowlers)
  ✘ Deep cover
              ✘ Cover                  ✘
                                    Mid-wicket


        Mid-off ✘         ■⊓        ✘ Mid-on
```

Fig. 10. Typical field for a 40-over limited innings

CHAPTER THIRTEEN

Equipment

Every time I return to South Africa to do my annual coaching stint, I am always surprised at the amount of money parents are willing to pay to have their sons instructed. At the same time I always feel that some of this money ought to have been spent on equipment. Whilst I am the first to admit that cricket gear is very expensive, it is sad to see so many youngsters waddling into the nets in boots three sizes too big, almost hidden behind gigantic pads and dragging a bat that has been bought to last them for four or five years.

So often we have to strip them of their brand new gear, which is a disappointment to them, and let them borrow something more appropriate. After the net, of course, they return home with their own kit and play with it. This can lead them into such bad habits that the net has almost been a waste of time.

Perhaps, then, I could begin talking about equipment with a plea to parents that it is much better to pass down second-hand gear of the right size to boys than to spend money on new kit which is relatively useless until they have finally grown into it.

The bat is the greatest source of nightmares for the coach. A schoolboy who has been given a bat he can hardly lift will immediately have problems with his grip. With a correct grip he just will not be able to lift it out of the blockhole. Instead he may stick his first finger down the back of the splice or hold his hands far apart; either method will serve no purpose when he grows older. He will be far better using a school bat until he graduates to his own.

The guideline for the correct size is that, stood alongside your leg, the bat should reach about three or four inches below the waist. Anything taller than that and it is becoming a little on the large side.

Having found a bat to suit you, you must of course treat it with care and attention. One thing I strongly advise you *not* to do is to stand it in linseed oil. There is a theory that this gives the bat durability, but from my experience the practice just clogs the bat up and makes it much heavier. Instead, apply a little sandpaper to the face after use and then add a light coating of oil to not only the face and the edges, but even to the back as well. If you have used it in very damp conditions, make sure you do a thorough job of cleaning it afterwards. As a last resort take out a razor blade and slice off any remaining flecks of dirt.

With a brand new bat, you must prepare it for use in the middle. I suggest oiling it once a week for about two months and knocking it in with a softish, old leather ball. Don't use a composition ball; it could split the surface. One excellent way to do this is to put the ball in an old sock and hang it from a clothes line or a tree; you now have an opportunity not only to break in your new bat but also to practise your shots. Don't neglect this preparation. The two months spent getting it ready for use should make the bat last at least six months longer.

In the last few years, manufacturers have produced a range of bats covered in synthetic materials that can be used the moment you take off the wrappings. I have started using them myself and they have worked well for me. By far the majority of bats, however, are still made of untreated willow and you must knock them in before any violent use.

As you graduate to senior cricket, the selection of the right bat is further complicated by the length of the handle. In choosing this you should be entirely dictated by comfort. The theory that the taller you are the longer should be your bat handle is only true for certain players. I am around six foot and I use a short handle. Tom Graveney, who is around the same height, also used one, whilst Richie Benaud, another six-footer, preferred a super-short. On the other hand, Asif Iqbal, the Pakistan and Kent all-rounder, prefers a long handle and he is well under six foot. Go for what feels comfortable to you. You'll never make runs if the bat doesn't feel right in your hands.

Size and comfort are also very important factors in the selection of pads. Cricket is all about making runs, and if you are peering over the top of massive leg-guards that almost reach your chin you are never going to be able to sprint up and down the wicket to make your score. There is a simple way to tell if they are the right fit for you. Most makes have extra padding for the knee, a criss-cross of protection. This should always be in front of your knee and not halfway up the thigh.

The best pads are those made of buckskin, but there are now plenty of cheaper varieties with a plastic finish. These wear well and have the extra advantage that you can clean them with soap and water.

Whilst oversized bats and pads certainly provide many coaches with headaches, gloves too can be a problem. Those used in senior cricket are usually of the 'sausage' variety with tubes of padding sewn along the backs of the fingers and the backs of the hands. If a youngster puts on a pair of these he finds that he can hardly bend his fingers, let alone grip the bat. The protection on these gloves is designed to safeguard the hands from bowling of the sort of pace that schoolboys will never be called on to face. Therefore the most sensible glove for a young player is the one made of light cotton with spiked rubber protection. These mould easily to the hand and there should be no problem about gripping the bat.

Of course at the later stages of a school career, the 'sausage' gloves should be used as the batsman becomes strong enough to use them and the bowlers are quick enough to demand greater protection for the hands.

The unwieldy nature of wicket-keeping gloves is less of a problem because the ball is not gripped with the same intensity as the bat. Nevertheless, as a young 'keeper you must be able to feel the ball to catch it at all, so once more size is very important. If you start out wearing adult gloves you will find that you can push three of your fingers into one finger hole so you will have little control over the movement of the gloves.

When you are trying on a pair for size, don't forget to slip on a pair of cotton inners. You must 'keep with inners on to cushion your hands, and they do fill out the gloves' insides. A lot of young 'keepers wet their inners before they go out to field. I cannot see the logic of this; all it does is wet the inside of the gloves and eventually rot them. A straightforward pair of cotton inners should serve your purpose admirably.

One final point about your gloves. The rippled rubber surface which covers the palms and fingers eventually wears flat and the surface becomes smooth. Just now and then balls will slip out of your hands that would have been retained by the rough, ripple surface. If you take the gloves to a sports shop, they can pull off the old surface and stick down a replacement. It's much cheaper than buying a new pair.

Still on size, try wherever possible to wear boots that are a comfortable fit. The greatest problem I find is that boots have been bought to last for two years on a growing boy and his feet are sliding around inside and blistering. If this has to happen, then two pairs of socks plus an inner sole do lessen the friction by reducing the space. Nevertheless comfort is so important when you are playing a lot of cricket that some professionals have a mould made of their feet and the boots made to measure.

These days boots come in a wide range of styles and soles. If you are a quick bowler, you should have a full boot that supports the ankle with studs and or spikes in the heel and sole. This will help relieve a little of the strain that the ankle and foot endures over a season. Even in schoolboy cricket I have seen pace bowlers drag their back foot, toe downwards, through the delivery stride. If you bowl in this style, ask your sports shop to fit a steel toecap on to the boot otherwise you will go through about three pairs a season.

Other players might find the low cut, soccer style boot lighter and easier to run around it, and I have used this style over the last few seasons. In England, because of the risk of damp conditions, these should have studs back and front. Even on the hottest day, there is always a chance of a little moisture on the grass before 12 o'clock, and it is just not worth the risk of slipping and pulling a muscle. In South Africa I have experimented with a boot that has the sprigs in the front but a rubber sole on the heel, but I finally discarded it because I slipped now and then. In really dry conditions some players prefer the lightness of a ripple sole boot, especially for batting, but it really does have to be dry to eliminate all risk of falling over. In New South Wales, these boots were banned after one or two players had slipped going for catches in Sheffield Shield games; this upset some of the side, but wearing unreliable footwear creates a totally unnecessary problem.

With most mothers possessing considerable dexterity with needle, and thread, shirts and flannels provide less of a problem. The accent here should be on cleanliness. Nothing looks worse than a side taking the field with half of them smeared in green around the knees and elbows. There is an old saying in cricket, 'If you can't be a cricketer, at least look like one.' And this is very true about all cricket clothing.

The trousers should be creased, and I think they look much smarter without a turn-up. Keep your shirts pressed, and if possible wear a cricket shirt as opposed to the ordinary white shirt. When you start to sweat on the field, the cricket shirt absorbs it so much better. Others stick to your back and eventually restrict movement.

Sweaters too should be clean and not creased. If your school team or club doesn't have a recognised sweater, it looks so much neater if you all wear plain white. It's not always possible, I know. When Hampshire play against Oxford and Cambridge Universities, the students always look a little disorganised because there are six or seven different sweaters on show, as only the 'blues' can wear the university sweater. Really it is like playing soccer. When you are all in the same kit, it somehow binds you together and makes you feel a team. Most sports shops stock plain white sweaters and I wouldn't be surprised if they are slightly cheaper than those with a coloured edging.

In South Africa and Australia, you can almost certainly make do with one sleeveless and one long-sleeve sweater. In England, I advise you to acquire as many as you can, because it can be bitterly cold in the field. I remember that at Northampton in 1972, I wore four – two short and two long.

The point about uniformity also applies to caps. Some players in the side may be entitled to one style of cap because of seniority, but the rest should try to wear the same. I am no great admirer, either, of the caps of a thousand colours that schoolboys seem to collect from their fathers' wardrobes. If you are going to wear a cap, it must also be a reasonable fit. If it keeps falling off when you run, you may as well leave it in the dressing-room.

One item of equipment many schoolboys frown upon is a protector. When the bowling is still not fast enough to cause a painful blow – and that only applies to the very young age groups – they may be right. But from then on my advice is always to wear one. The pink plastic variety that you can slip easily into athletic support is light, comfortable and strong. If you are ever hit batting without one you will never make that mistake again; it really can be very nasty. If you are asked to field close to the bat, particularly in front of the wicket, don't be ashamed to ask the twelfth man to bring a protector out for you.

Whilst I have emphasised that it is important to wear equipment that is comfortable, it is also equally vital that you can transport all the items from ground to ground in comfort. With most of the items being either heavy or of an awkward size, the right style of cricket bag is essential. Nothing could be worse than battling on a train or a bus to a match with a hold-all in each hand and your pads strapped around your head!

One style which is perfectly adequate is the long hold-all that has a compartment for sliding in your bat. This will be perfectly sufficient as you start your cricket life, but as you gather more and more items of equipment, you may find you need something larger. A lot of county cricketers in England settle for a suitcase or a small trunk. Quite often we are travelling for a week or ten days and we have to take enough kit to cover play on each day.

The major alternative is what is known as a club bag, the sort that your school kit is probably taken in, used as a personal carry-all. I can tell you from experience that if you do have a bag large enough to take all your gear you stand a far smaller chance of losing the odd item. If you have half your kit in a duffle bag and the rest in a small hold-all, you never know what is where.

I have emphasised that cricket gear is very expensive. If you are at school, probably most of it has come to you as presents from generous relations. Don't abuse their kindness. Take care of every item you possess. Make it last as long as possible. At the end of the summer, clean all your gear thoroughly before you put it away. Give the bat a final sandpaper and a liberal oiling. Clean the boots thoroughly with whitening and pick the sprigs clean. Have all the clothing cleaned and pressed. Remember, your equipment is vital to your success. Treat it kindly.

CHAPTER FOURTEEN

Approach to the Game

The way to enjoy your cricket to the full is to be successful at it. There will be times when the bounce of the ball goes against you; this will happen to everybody. Yet at the end of the season, you will have justified the time you have given to the game if you can look back on a season of success.

How well you do on the cricket field lies in your own hands. In the previous chapters I have outlined techniques for all phases of the game, most of which have proved over the years to be basic styles adopted by those who have reached the higher levels. Obviously, any natural ability you do possess will be a great help, but try to channel this skill into the correct techniques. From there – and I have emphasised this time after time throughout the book – practice becomes paramount.

Cricket is never an easy game, and its very nature soon deflates the egos of those who do not put in the hours of preparation. The way the first class game is going at the moment, with the emphasis on limited-over cricket, the player who can participate in every aspect has become extremely valuable. The batsman who can bowl quite tidily and field well is a basic constituent of the side. Bowlers, too, are often required to make runs under the pressures of a thrilling finish. This never happened years ago when numbers ten and eleven enjoyed themselves with a carefree slog. Now versatility is vital and it is not a quality that appears overnight. Regular practice brings its own rewards.

Approach to the Game

As far as batting is concerned, the nets can be particularly useful for you to cultivate your attacking shots. I suppose I have built my reputation on playing a few strokes, but I don't think this is beyond any player. To win matches, your side must score runs, and as a batsman this is your job. Sometimes it will be in the interests of the team to defend, but I don't believe that there are quite so many of these occasions as some players would have you believe.

By adopting an attacking attitude, I don't mean that you are looking to whack every ball for four. But I do think that young players should aim to score off as many balls as possible. In county cricket in particular, far too many deliveries are allowed to pass unpunished. I firmly believe that if there is a bad ball bowled to you, whether it is the first ball of the innings or the last delivery before lunch, you should try to hit it for runs. Don't block it just because it happens to be bowled just before an interval or before the close of play. Far too many bowlers are allowed to get away with moderate bowling because the batsmen are concentrating on defence rather than attack. Of course, you will find that you are out more often, but at the same time there should be far more runs to your name in the score-book.

I quite appreciate that some batsmen, the 'grafters' or 'workers' we call them in first-class cricket, do not have the range of strokes to tear an attack apart. But really this is no excuse for adopting a defensive attitude. If you come into this category, you can still keep the score moving by looking for singles and sprinting between the wickets. In schoolboy cricket and even at higher levels, so many runs are wasted, because the players do not assess the situation sharply enough.

This is not a fault that you could ever apply to Doug Walters. I am sure that anyone who has watched him play will consider him an attacking player. And he is, but not because he hits a tremendous number of runs in boundaries. A typical Walters century would probably come in around two and a half hours, which is quicker than par, and yet he would only have hit eight or nine boundaries. This is because he looks to score off every ball; if he receives a good delivery he will settle for defence, but anything less and it's runs for him. He had a disappointing time in England in 1972, yet his record over the years has been very consistent. There are very few balls which he should score off that he doesn't.

This brings us back to my pet philosophy about placing the ball through the field. You can crack the ball with all your might to a fielder and get no runs, but a delicately placed shot into a space will add to your score. This rule was drummed into me in my early years with the Tech College club in Durban by Trevor Goddard. He always used to say, 'If you can't hit the ball really hard to beat the field, you have got to put it where there aren't any fielders.' And I have tried very hard to heed his words.

Another more general point that requires re-emphasising is concentration on the field. I don't mean that you must change your personality. Concentration comes in different forms. A player like Clive Radley, always bustling about, catches the eye with his restless enthusiasm. But this is his style of play and it reflects the type of man he is. I sometimes receive criticism because I don't show the same extrovert interest. Standing at slip, I often find myself accused of being disinterested, but nothing is further from the truth. Graeme Pollock is another who seems to have his mind on other things in the field, but you rarely see him misfield the ball or drop a catch. As long as you are concentrating, you are doing your job.

One way I have altered my personality, as I have played more cricket, is in my reaction to failure. At every level you will find players who mope around the dressing-room or who lock themselves away after they have been bowled for nought. I was one of the many, even up until my first season with Hampshire. It was so important to me to make runs that I found it very difficult to come to terms with the times that I failed.

But slowly, as I suppose I matured as a person, I grew more philosophical. I realised that there was no use getting upset if someone had bowled me a great delivery. It had happened and that was that. I couldn't go back out again.

Approach to the Game

It is still very important that I score runs, but I think I have learned to be able to enjoy the game even if things haven't quite gone according to plan. If you are a 'moper', I sympathise and I am far from critical of you. But I think the nature of the game is such that no one can succeed all the time, so it is better to be able to cope emotionally when it is not your day.

However, it is very unhealthy to finish on a note about failure. What every cricketer is striving for is success. The recipe always sounds so simple on paper. It is never quite that easy. But I hope that by following my advice and taking the techniques into the nets with you, you will emerge a much better player. I have been fortunate enough to experience an endless amount of pleasure from playing cricket. I am sure that if you work at your game you will be able to experience much of it for yourself.

Index

Arnold, Geoff, 24, 71, 72

Bacher, Ali, 14, 88–9
back foot, attack off, 41–50
  defence off, 20, 22–5, 26
backlift, 16, 17, 21, 29, 30
Barrington, Ken, 15
ball, seam, use of, 74–5
  shine on, 69
Barlow, Eddie, 90
bat, size of, 114–15 *See also* batting
batting:
  awareness of fielders' positions, 19, 33, 122
  backlift, 16, 17, 21, 29, 30
  comfort during, 13–19
  grip, 13, 14
  grounding, 55
  stance, 14–15
  taking guard, 18
  see also under individual shots
Benaud, Richie, 78, 79, 82, 85, 86
Bijl, Vincent van der, 66
Bland, Colin, 98, 100
bouncer, 76, 77
bowler, demoralisation by batsman, 28, 35, 37

bowling, 60–92
  accuracy, 62, 65–6
  action, 60–5
  demoralisation of batsman, 76–7, 87–90
  fast bowling, 61–3, 68–77
  field for, 70, 73, 111
  line of attack, 71–3
  polishing ball, 69
  seam bowling, 79
  slow bowling, 62, 63, 78–86
  field for, 79, 80, 81, 83, 112
  slower ball, 75–7
  spin bowling, 78–86
  swing bowling, 69–74
  see also under individual shots
Boycott, Geoff, 13, 20
Bradman, Sir Donald, 25, 47

captaincy, responsibilities of, 107–11
  batting order, 110
  change of bowlers, 108
  discipline on field, 109
  setting of fielders, 108
  study of field positions, 107
  team spirit, 111
Cartwright, Tom, 64
Castell, Alan, 82

Index

Chappell, Greg, 14, 46, 82
Chappell, Ian, 46, 89, 94, 109, 111
Close, Brian, 95
comfort in crease, 13–19
  stance, 14–15
concentration, 52, 53, 122
Cowdrey, Colin, 30, 40
cut, 41, 48
  late, 48
  square, 49

Davidson, Alan, 15
defensive technique, 20–7
  backward, 20, 22–5, 26
  forward, 20, 21–2, 23, 26, 36
  practice, 22, 24
D'Oliveira, Basil, 16, 40
drive, 28–37
  balance, 31
  cover-drive, 32
  follow-through, 30
  going down the wicket, 34–5, 36
  lofted drive, 34
  on-drive, 32, 33
  practice, 36

Edrich, John, 14, 77
Edwards, Ross, 98
Engineer, Farookh, 35
equipment, 113–19
  bat, 113
  boots, 116–17
  cap, 118
  cricket bag, 118–19
  flannels, 117
  gloves, 115
    wicket-keeping gloves, 115–16
  shirt, 117
  sweater, 117–18
  pads, 115
  protector, 118

failure, coping with, 122–3
fielding techniques, 93–100
  close fielding, 95, 96, 98, 122
    catching, 96
  gully, 95
  outfielding, 98
    catching, 98–9
    return to 'keeper, 99
  practice, 96–7, 100
  short leg, 95
  slip, 94
  specialisation in one position, 93

Gamsy, Denis, 94
Goddard, Trevor, 17, 90, 122
googly, 83, 84
Grace, W. G., 13
Graveney, Tom, 26, 115

Hall, Wes, 76
hook, 41, 44–6, 50

Illingworth, Ray, 62, 66
innings, building, 51–9
  concentration, 52, 53
  playing oneself in, 53
  study of bowler, 58
Intikhab Alam, 82
Iqbal, Asif, 115
Irvine, Lee, 56

Jesty, Trevor, 94

Knott, Alan, 34, 102, 103, 104

Laker, Jim, 81, 86
Larwood, Harold, 76
Lawry, Bill, 24
l.b.w. rule, 72
leg cutter, 74
leg glance, 37–9, 40, 43
  opening the face, 38–9
Lillee, Dennis, 24, 26, 61

Index

limited-over cricket, 53, 102, 111–12
Lindsay, Denis, 104
Lloyd, Clive, 98

Mackay-Coghill, Don, 97
Massie, Bob, 71, 74
May, Peter, 57
McGlew, Jackie, 90, 107, 110, 111
McKenzie, Graham, 24
Merwe, Peter van der, 111
Mohammad, Mushtaq, 82

off cutter, 75
Old, Chris, 68

Parfitt, Peter, 109
Parks, Jim, 102
Pollock, Graeme, 13, 22, 25, 33, 41, 122
Pollock, Peter, 17, 45, 66, 77
Price, John, 61
Procter, Mike, 17, 18, 22, 24, 26, 46, 58, 60, 61, 64, 68, 76, 77, 89, 107, 110
pull, 41, 46–8

Radley, Clive, 56, 122
Roope, Graham, 32, 94
run-getting, 33, 54
   calling, 54
   study of fielders, 33, 54, 122

Sainsbury, Peter, 37
Sheahan, Paul, 98
Short, Arthur, 32
Smith, Mike, 37
Snow, John, 17, 26, 37, 46, 60, 61, 66, 68, 74, 77
Sobers, Gary, 13, 16, 22
spin bowling, 78–86
   change of pace, 84
   delivery, 80, 81, 83
   googly, 83, 84

   left arm, 81
   leg break, 78, 82, 84
   off spin, 79
   practice, 86
   top spin, 78, 83
Stackpole, Keith, 45
Stephenson, Bob, 94
Stewart, Micky, 39
Sweep, 39–40
swing bowling, 69–74
   inswing, 72
   outswing, 70–2

talking on the field, 109
Tayfield, Hugh, 86
temperament, 51–2, 122
Trueman, Fred, 77
Trumper, Victor, 13
Tyson, Frank, 17

Underwood, Derek, 62, 66, 90

Walters, Doug, 121
wicket-keeping, 101–6
   agility, 101, 105
   concentration, 105
   position of hands, 103
   practice, 102, 105
   standing back, 103, 105
   standing up, 104, 105
   stumping, 105
   taking the ball, 102
wicket-taking (bowler), 87–92
   correct field placing, 89, 90
   fitness, 91–2
   making use of pitch conditions, 91
   spotting opponents' weaknesses, 87–8
   which end to bowl, 90
Willis, Bob, 68
Wilkins, Chris, 89
'working the ball', 37

yorker, 72, 77, 85